BUILDING A LOG CABIN RETREAT

MICHAEL MULLIGAN

BUILDING A LOG CABIN RETREAT

A DO-IT-YOURSELF GUIDE

PALADIN PRESS · BOULDER, COLORADO

Building a Log Cabin Retreat: A Do-It-Yourself Guide
by Michael Mulligan

Copyright © 2002 by Michael Mulligan

ISBN 1-58160-314-2
Printed in the United States of America

Published by Paladin Press, a division of
Paladin Enterprises, Inc.
Gunbarrel Tech Center
7077 Winchester Circle
Boulder, Colorado 80301 USA
+1.303.443.7250

Direct inquiries and/or orders to the above address.

PALADIN, PALADIN PRESS, and the "horse head" design
are trademarks belonging to Paladin Enterprises and
registered in United States Patent and Trademark Office.

Visit our Web site at www.paladin-press.com

Table of Contents

Why Build a Cabin in the Forest?

It was the best of times, it was the worst of times, it was the age of wisdom, it was the age of foolishness, it was the epoch of belief, it was the epoch of incredulity, it was the season of Light, it was the season of Darkness, it was the spring of hope, it was the winter of despair, we had everything before us, we had nothing before us . . . it was clearer than crystal to the lords of the State preserves of loaves and fishes, that things in general were settled for ever.

—Charles Dickens
A Tale of Two Cities

So wrote that most perceptive of authors in the year 1859 about the year 1775 when the French Revolution was about to splinter European society. Today, as we engage in a new kind of warfare against terrorists whose worldview is as foreign to us as the landscape of Mars, we see that our own "best of times" was rife with similar contradictions.

In the wake of the terrorist attacks of September 11, 2001, the heroic and skillful actions of our military, law enforcement, and public safety personnel have ignited a spirit of unity and resolve for which we will continue to owe them a growing debt of gratitude. Cultural clashes of this magnitude are never resolved quickly. It will be a long fight, and the actions taken by both sides are sure to be replete with unintended consequences. And so, as we brace ourselves for a protracted battle on the terrorist front, we must remain ever vigilant against an ongoing legacy of political and administrative insiders using their posts to further causes and agendas that are dubious at best. Minimizing the insidious erosive effect of the latter on our freedoms remains essential to preserving our way of life, and it is something we will touch on from time to time in this book as we examine the ins and outs of a log cabin project.

In such uncertain times, wherein the bizarre and the unanticipated are a matter of course and "homeland security" no longer is, a log cabin in a remote location is a particularly nice thing to have. The chapters that follow offer guidance in the creation of a remote cabin, suitable for vacations and hunting, with some essential extras—things that make it double as an emergency retreat. Even if an urgent need for such a retreat does not arise, building a log cabin is a highly rewarding activity in its own right.

The focus of this book is a do-it-yourself project using improvised materials. Of course, anyone wishing to spend substantial sums of money could easily have the things described here built on a much larger and grander scale. However, that route bypasses a very important aspect of surviving an upheaval in relative comfort (if at all): the development of your own human capital and adaptability. Such things are far more important than mere money when things get tough. Of course, the projects covered here do cost money, and a person with absolutely no discretionary funds would not be in a position to start out on them. But doing the most with the smallest possible expenditure is what human capital development is all about. One of the worst things about a period of accelerating prosperity is that people are apt to forget how to do things with skill and economy. And when everybody does that, the prosperity quickly dissipates.

So we shall examine the preparation of a private camping site where one could remain for a short time on vacation or a much longer time under duress. An essential element of the site is secrecy. It should exist in an area that is fairly remote without bordering on inaccessibility. The centerpiece of the camping site is a log cabin. Another sort of building would surely do the job, but the log cabin is an excellent project to develop building skills as well as the ability to adapt and improvise. It is also an object that many people find extremely attractive in its own right. The American pioneer tradition of log cabin living remains strong even in today's high-tech world.

The next chapter will offer some insight on finding the right piece of land on which to build a log cabin intended to serve as a campsite *and* an emergency retreat and discuss the ins and outs of purchasing that land. The remainder of the book will focus on the cabin itself, examining the following subjects in depth:

- **Construction:** How do you select and prepare the logs, lay out the foundation, and build a log cabin from the ground up?
- **Utilities:** How can you obtain the sorts of things we take for granted in cities and suburbs (e.g., drinking water, sewage disposal, power, and light) in a way that retains the desired level of secrecy and also remains operative in the event that the flow of consumer supplies is interrupted?
- **Scaled-up versions:** If you should decide to build something bigger, what are some of the structural issues you must consider when using logs straight from the forest?
Everything described in this book has been done, built,

lived in, and tested for significant periods of time. All of it requires a degree of skill, but it is a degree that any dedicated amateur can attain.

A project like this is never really finished, so all one can do is make a start on what will undoubtedly be a long journey. From there, a project of this kind takes on a life of its own. A little bit of accomplishment always serves as the spark that ignites the ambition needed to pull off the next step.

Perhaps you're thinking, "Oh that would be nice, but I haven't got that kind of money." Are you sure? Most people could have a lot more spare money if they examined their spending habits closely. Those elaborate home entertainment centers and video rentals are really just numbing their minds for long hours every day, making them all the more susceptible to clever advertising campaigns designed to convince them that various products are practically indispensable, when really they're not. Advertising agencies are masters at creating bandwagons that consumers hop on just because they are there, rather than for good reason. Their marketing ploys are particularly effective on young people, who then become adults without ever really changing their buying habits.

Consider that *half* of the retail price of many of the small, repeat-purchase products we buy is devoted to national advertising. One product, in particular, illustrates this fact and uses it to its own advantage. It is a brand of sunscreen called NO-AD, for "not advertised." NO-AD can be found on store shelves, particularly in large chain stores, right beside nationally advertised competitors such as Coppertone. The prices of the two products are comparable, but the unadvertised product is in a container that holds twice as much. In general, you can find substitute brands for most of the heavily advertised products you buy somewhere—though perhaps not always on the adjacent shelf and not always stating their case as plainly as NO-AD does. It's worth thinking about.

There is a whole parallel distribution system for discounted products that most consumers never notice. There are stores that sell discounted groceries comprised of odd lots, slightly dented cans, creased breakfast cereal boxes with intact inner bags, paper products with ripped packages, and all manner of serviceable but slightly unattractive items. The same goes for slightly imperfect clothing. These discount stores might not have a complete line of goods conducive to one-stop shopping, but when used intelligently they can generate loads of spare cash. In the same way, yard sales present fantastic money-saving opportunities.

To some, it may seem odd to suggest that seemingly pedestrian items bought at bargain prices can lead to the wherewithal to buy substantial amounts of rural land, something that is particularly difficult to finance. If you are among them, please take a look at *The Millionaire Next Door* by T.J. Stanley and W.D. Danko. The authors, two business school professors who are experts in marketing, have researched very carefully the patterns of behavior that lead to wealth accumulation, and their findings are quite illuminating. The recurring theme is day-to-day frugality.

The important thing to bear in mind is that money is a mere medium of exchange, while wealth is what money can buy. And wealth has to be created, ultimately through the application of thoughtful effort put forth by somebody. That somebody should be you, not some anonymous seller. A vacation cabin hidden in a forest is an excellent example of wealth.

Chapter 1

Buying
Your Land

By the shores of Gitche Gumee,
By the shining Big-Sea-Water,
Stood the wigwam of Nokomis,
Daughter of the Moon, Nokomis,
Dark behind it rose the forest . . .

—Henry Wadsworth Longfellow
The Song of Hiawatha

Hiawatha lived around 1570. The rural real estate market has undergone some remarkable changes since then.

If your cabin is to maintain its retreat function, it must remain out of sight. Ideally, its existence would remain unknown to all local people. If emergency conditions were to arise and you were to need it as a retreat, various local people might need it too, and they're in a position to get to it first. Also, there are some more bureaucratic reasons we might

1

have to keep the cabin entirely out of sight, which I will discuss shortly.

Figure 1-1 shows an entrance to the kind of land we're looking for. It is a completely unremarkable entrance to a narrow lane that holds no particular appeal for wanderers and snoopers. Nothing of interest can be seen. There is a locked, farm-type gate and enough side fencing to make it very inconvenient to go around. There is no mailbox, and the only sign says, "No Trespassing." Comings and goings are not particularly noticeable to anyone.

LET'S GO SHOPPING

The task of finding the remote cabin site you want is like looking for a lost object. There appears to be no end in sight

Figure 1-1: An entrance to our kind of campsite.

until you find just the right deal. But all that unsuccessful turmoil then becomes a useful asset, since you will need a substantial background of real estate knowledge to recognize just the right deal when you do come across it. If the very first thing you look at seems to be the right deal, you're probably wrong. Many real estate agents post listings at unreasonably high prices in the hope that some naive soul with too much money will fall into the trap. These properties sit and sit on the market until that naive soul buys or until the seller eventually needs some money and gets realistic. Only through the experience of lots of shopping will you be able to tell the difference between a good deal and a bad one. The real estate agent won't offer any insight; he or she works for the seller. However, the agent is prohibited from refusing to transmit a low-ball offer you might make to the seller.

The term "recreational property" is a recognizable category in the real estate business. In keeping with the objective of keeping the cabin project a secret, you need not get much more specific than "private campsite" with regard to your intended use of the property as you deal with brokers and salespeople. Real estate agents don't want to alienate customers, but they also are rather close to talkative and snoopy local courthouse bureaucrats as a matter of their business. They might even bring you into the "lion's den" to look at courthouse records with them. This is all right. Just let the boring people you will meet there continue doing their boring jobs, and avoid small talk.

When you approach a real estate agent, remember that the kind of property you are looking for is probably a fairly small listing among many others that have existing houses on them. Real estate agents burn a lot of time and gasoline taking prospects to listed properties, especially in the kind of remote areas we are interested in. You and your relatively small prospective sale will get a lot more serious attention if you discuss the kinds of things you want at the office first, drive out for a cursory and unhurried look at various listings by your-self next, and then ask the agent to show you around only those properties that look particularly interesting.

Real estate agents had private dial-up computer listing services for accessing distant markets long before the Internet became popular. Now, with the World Wide Web, you can do some preliminary searches yourself. Search engines seem to respond well to the words "real estate" coupled with the name of a particular region. You can usually find some sites that have listings with asking prices. These will help you gauge how high prices are running in a particular locality, but they are not likely to be exhaustive lists. Classified ads in the news-papers of distant towns and local real estate association hand-outs are also valuable resources. Although none of these are likely to feature prominently what you are looking for, they are good sources of talking points to use when contacting a real estate agency.

Once you've gotten down to inspecting a particular piece of property, there are some invisible things to beware of. Property deeds sometimes include things called "easements," which are passed on from owner to owner and are rarely elim-inated from property deeds. They are provisions for others to have some specific use of your property. Utility lines are the most common. If an overhead utility line passes through your property then the easement gives the utility company (or con-tractors it has hired) the right to enter the property in order to maintain its facilities and to cut trees that might interfere with the wires. Occasionally, an easement exists to allow an adja-cent property owner "ingress and egress" rights through the parcel. Obviously, such easements reduce your privacy, not to mention the fact that actually trying to subscribe to a utility amounts to a dead giveaway of your cabin's existence. Utilities *will* rat to the courthouse. They are part of a regulat-ed industry, practically an arm of the government. As you will see later, you can do without them anyway.

Another "poison pill" sometimes found in a deed is a "covenant." Usually associated with exclusive subdivisions, covenants are legally binding rules that landowners must follow. Typically they specify the style of home you must build—something like, "Colonial, no less than 2,500 square feet." Sometimes they prohibit high fences or other types of landscaping. You wouldn't expect such things on the kinds of remote lands we are talking about, but there is always a possibility that some long-forgotten, unsuccessful development project attached covenants to all the deeds. Be sure to ask before you sign on the dotted line.

LEGAL ADVICE

I am not a lawyer. I do, on occasion, advise consulting a lawyer, and finalizing a land deal of any kind is definitely such an occasion. Land is called "real property" and is viewed by the legal system quite differently than other kinds of ownership. In particular, you own a piece of land only when a legally binding description of the property, or "deed," bearing your name is properly recorded at the local courthouse. And a transfer of ownership should not take place until the seller has cleared any liens that might be on record against that property. Liens may be the result of unpaid taxes or other bills, a contested will, or the like. A licensed attorney with specific real estate experience is the only person qualified to handle this kind of ownership transfer. And this attorney should advise you to purchase the property in "fee simple" (outright purchase for cash—possibly borrowed, but cash). If not, consider finding another lawyer.

One type of purchase you should always avoid is called a "land contract." Land contracts are occasionally offered on the kinds of remote parcels where you might want to build a cabin, and if you want the property you should try to get the seller to agree to fee simple or else drop the deal. A land contract is a private contract under which you agree to make payments as you would do for a mortgage, but the actual title transfer at the courthouse doesn't occur until you've made all of the payments. Bad deal! Why? Two reasons: First, what if you fail to make a payment on time? The delinquency might be the result of a lost letter at the post office, or you might be temporarily out of money for some reason. Regardless, the seller is still entitled to the payment. In the case of a dispute, the seller has all of your previous payments and still has ownership of the property. You are in a bad position. You could lose your money and the land too. Secondly, even when the buyer makes all the payments, title transfer doesn't occur until that last payment has been made. What if the seller doesn't really have a clear title? Maybe there were no liens at the beginning of the payment process but something happened in the meantime. You and the lawyer you've hired won't know until it's too late. If there is a title problem, the seller should be compelled to give you the money back . . . *if* he still has it. Sometimes the seller turns out to be an empty shell of a corporation that has long since paid out your money to its employees/owners. The land contract is a big trap. Maybe it has even been baited with a "no down payment" offer. Stay out!

With a fee-simple deal (your jurisdiction may have a different but equivalent name for it), you get title transfer right away. The property may have a new lien on it because of all the loan payments you haven't made yet, but the title is in *your* name. If you do have a payment problem later on, having the title in your own name gives you some wiggle room to avoid catastrophic loss of money—even if you have to sell the property quickly.

Buying rural land with mortgage payments is difficult. Banks are not given to granting loans on unimproved land. Sometimes a seller offers to be the lender. There are tax advantages that might motivate him to do so. But be careful. If the seller seems too anxious to be the lender, you should try to find out why. Perhaps this land is part of some kind of subdivision that will quickly give you more neighbors than you really want. Be wary. Maybe you have family that would be willing to grant you that loan. Maybe, through day-to-day frugality, you can save enough money to buy the property outright.

ILLEGAL ADVICE

Before we go seeking land deals or loan money or even that real estate lawyer, let us reflect upon some hard facts of life. The freedoms we enjoy as Americans are increasingly under siege, threatened not only by outside forces but also from within. Laws, ordinances, regulations, and bureaucratic processes have crept into our daily lives, often unnoticed, and often with our blessing in the name of "heightened security." Building a campsite on your own land including a small log cabin that is not a residence and is not in view of anybody may appear to be a perfectly normal, beneficial, and healthful All-American thing to do. So it is, but it may be against the law. If so, and if it comes to the attention of the wrong people in your local courthouse, they may very well seek and obtain a court order to have it bulldozed. The difficulty is that many states have authorized localities to pass building codes. This is supposed to be done to protect the buying public from unsafe or poorly built housing. The localities usually respond by (1) adopting a pre-existing code formulated by an "association" of "experts" and (2) hiring a building inspector, or "building official," as they are usually designated within this adopted code. Building contractors, plumbers, and electricians must all do their work under the aegis of this official, who sees to it that all regulatory provisions of the code are met. Trouble is, the code, which is now local law, gives vast authority to this "building official" character, who, given the kinds of salaries that localities are likely to pay, is under-qualified at best and always works in a rigid, stratified, and thoroughly bureaucratic courthouse environment. And while the provisions of the code are usually reasonable for ordinary building projects, most simply don't provide for the kind of hunting cabin we're talking about at all. If you try to get a building permit for a tiny log hunting cabin, local building officials will likely insist on calling it a full-scale residence and require you to include everything a new house must have under the code, right down to the washer-drier installation. When in doubt, a building official always says "no," and backs up that "no" with legal threats, usually in writing and on record.

Sound far-fetched? I wish it were. But you must consider the kinds of personalities involved. As I mentioned in the Preface, this kind of project involves the creation of wealth— that is, creating something of value that didn't exist before. Most public officials never, ever think in such terms. Lawyers, judges, politicians, and bureaucrats do not create wealth; they redistribute it, taking a big cut for themselves. To them, there is something vaguely wrong with creativity of any kind. They can't do it, others can, and that threatens their perception of their own importance. Worst of all are the judges. If you appear before one of them, you're already practically dead. Their hero, Oliver Wendell Holmes, once thundered down from the bench of the Supreme Court, "Young man, this is a court of *law*, not of justice!" And most of those laws weren't even written by (supposedly) accessible elected officials but rather by various interested parties who contribute heavily to election campaigns.

Sound hopeless? Actually, no. Given the wooden mind-set of these people, you can evade the system quite easily and with reasonable safety. The main rule is to avoid any impact on their feelings of self-importance. That's all that matters to them—not you the taxpayer, not the well-being of the community, just themselves. They're our enemies, but they're also little worms. Courthouse bureaucrats do not leave their desks to go out on search-and-destroy missions. They lie in wait for inquiries from naive citizens and occasionally respond to some complaint from a busybody neighbor. To do otherwise would require initiative—and people with initiative do not become bureaucrats. I once heard some scuttlebutt about an owner of a hunting cabin whose secret building had been discovered by a game warden searching for some feral dogs. The warden was said to have reported it to the building official, who then took legal action. This did not fit the pattern of bureaucratic life as I had come to know it, so I set out to find the owner and get the story firsthand. Like most scuttlebutt, it turned out to have a germ of truth but was mostly distortion. Yes, the cabin's owner did have a run-in with courthouse scum, and yes, he did have to hire an expensive lawyer to save his property. But a game warden did not find it and rat. The owner, thinking himself a good citizen, had gone to the courthouse himself, seeking an unrelated permit. He wanted to erect some permanent privies in order to host regularly scheduled shooting matches. Privies of any kind had been outlawed in the county (although large numbers of them still existed), and in an ensuing argument the owner let slip the existence of the hunting cabin. In the end, his lawyer saved the cabin by reaching a compromise with the building inspector: An independent contractor would inspect the cabin so as to grade the lumber from which it had been built, which was not previously graded. The inspector would accept the word of the contractor as to the suitability of the lumber. Building inspectors always seem to have a trusting relationship with local contractors. This does not necessarily mean that the contractors are good. It just means that as businessmen wanting to stay in business they have learned how to assuage the egos of these totally untalented courthouse denizens. Monetary payoffs are relatively rare. Contractors skillfully dispense something money could never buy for these people: self-respect. All the above lumber-grading exercise did was help the inspector fool himself into believing that he and his official position were really worth something.

The extent to which you may have to evade local regulations varies enormously from jurisdiction to jurisdiction. Some localities actually have a "log cabin law" exempting do-it-yourself home-building projects (which needn't really be a log cabin) from inspection requirements. Other places offer exemptions for buildings below a certain size that may apply to what you want to build. The worst places (which sometimes are very remote and thinly populated) are hugely restrictive, requiring extensive paperwork and "permission" for anything bigger than a doghouse.

Just asking in person at the courthouse about what kind of regulatory regime you might be facing can be hazardous. Courthouse people in remote jurisdictions usually have a wary eye for "strangers," and they have an especially keen sense for situations where they can unduly exert their authority. If you really want to know, a good starting place might be to have some trusted third party ask about regulations pertaining to erecting the kind of storage shed sold prefabricated by building supply stores. Your inquirer should avoid mentioning what the building is really for, particularly the fact that there might be some kind of toilet in it or that someone might be staying overnight in it.

And also, be cautious about what you say to your own lawyer about your plans. Yes, lawyers will do all they can for you once you're in legal difficulty, be it anything from a traffic ticket to a felony charge, but they won't conspire with you ahead of time to break the law. That could result in their being disbarred, eliminating *their* only ticket to self-esteem.

Since emergency retreats should be kept discrete, you might opt to forget about regulations entirely and keep your cabin secret from all locals.

Chapter 2
Building a Log Cabin

The sudden sight of a house on the edge of the path struck her like the shock of an unexpected sound: built in loneliness, cut off from all ties to human existence, it looked like the secret retreat of some great defiance or sorrow. It was the humblest home of the valley, a log cabin beaten in dark streaks by the tears of many rains, only its great windows withstanding the storms with the smooth, shining, untouched serenity of glass.

—Ayn Rand
Atlas Shrugged

Writing in the 1940s and '50s, novelist and philosopher Ayn Rand explored the all-too-familiar kind of political thinking that leads to disaster and upheaval and also anticipated most of the economic dangers that we face today. In her novel *Atlas Shrugged*, she even incorporated the kind of log cabin we address in this book: the *small* log cabin, valuable as a hidden retreat.

In keeping with the goals of inconspicuousness and economy, the inside floor areas of our cabin will be in the 200-square-foot range (although the structure can certainly be scaled up to a much larger size, the engineering issues of which are addressed in Chapter 4). I sincerely recommend building a smaller structure for practice before undertaking a larger project. I will explain what I can about log cabin building in this book, but some aspects of it must be experienced firsthand.

This chapter will discuss, in turn, the following nine steps to creating a basic log cabin:

- Planning and general layout
- Selecting and preparing the logs
- Preparing the foundation and platform
- Fabricating boxes for windows and doors

Figure 2-1: The sort of log cabin discussed in this book.

- Erecting log walls
- Building a roof
- Chinking the log walls
- Incorporating a chimney
- Finishing the interior

PLANNING AND GENERAL LAYOUT

Since a log cabin has no siding, your general plan must provide for features that will protect the logs from exposure to rain, wind, and ground moisture, all of which hasten decay. I once saw a wonderful log cabin, built about 50 years previously on what must have seemed, at the time, a perfect site. It was situated on a high bluff overlooking a wide river. Unfortunately, wind-driven rain had swept across the river and badly deteriorated the front wall logs, while the back and side walls remained standing in like-new condition. The lesson: situate your cabin so that it's surrounded by wind-breaking trees and shrubs, such as cedars and holly, which will shield it from both the elements and prying eyes year round. (Obviously, a bluff, with its high visibility, is contrary to our purposes here.)

At roughly the same time this cabin was being built, another log cabin project was underway nearby. An historic mansion was being refurbished and opened to the public, and since much work had to be done in a remote location, the project planners constructed a log cabin village to house the workers. This was during the Great Depression, so the village was built at very low cost. Project managers used an expedient log building technique without corner notches (which I will discuss later), and they projected the rear of many of the cabins over the edges of large gullies, thereby utilizing a location that would otherwise have had little value. When the workers had finished and left, these cabins became prized possessions of the mansion's board of directors and were later rented out to visitors. When the cabins later began to show signs of decay, management had to take some immediate steps to keep them operational. The worst problem was that the original cabins lacked both rain gutters and effective runoff control. Piles of leaves would collect on the sun decks that had been appended to many of the cabins, subjecting log walls to prolonged periods of wetness. Perched on piers at the edges of their gullies, many cabins had front lawns that sloped down to the front of the building, which in turn lacked sufficient ground clearance to prevent wet leaves from collecting in piles against the lower logs and causing decay. Fortunately, corrective action saved the cabins. When one cabin was destroyed in an accidental fire, management learned firsthand how expensive a modern, commercially made log cabin replacement was and became well motivated to properly maintain those that remained. Some initial planning for cabin longevity (which really wasn't a priority at the time the cabins were built) could have prevented this whole scenario of expense and lessons learned the hard way.

The simple schematic in Figure 2-2(a) illustrates what must be done to keep a log cabin safe from decay. Although the illustration depicts an eavesdrop, rain gutters are an excellent addition if the cabin will be visited often enough to keep them clear of leaves. Wood decay is caused by fungus, and fungus cannot grow below a threshold amount of water content—about 20 percent. Most species of log, when supported away from ground moisture and reasonably well sheltered from rain, will dry out to a level below the threshold needed to support fungus growth, thereby escaping decay. An occasional spattering of rain will quickly dry up as long as there are no moisture traps.

Telephone poles and railroad ties, which must contact the ground, undergo an artificial method of preservation: they are treated under high pressure with toxic chemicals that prevent fungus growth for many years. Eventually, though, these chemicals leach out and decay sets in. A well-planned and maintained log cabin will outlast ties and telephone poles many times over. Although some decay-inhibiting stains and preservatives brushed on the exterior of a log cabin are useful, thoroughly permeating toxic compounds are not in order for a cabin that is to be occupied. And they are not necessary. A stone or brick foundation that elevates the logs 18 inches above ground will keep ground moisture away. Because a full 18-inch foundation can look out of proportion on a small cabin, I like the compromise of a 12-inch foundation, using treated lumber for floor joists and a decay-resistant species of tree for the lowest course of logs (details follow later).

Occasionally one sees a log cabin built with bark left on the logs. This expedient is worthwhile only for a very rough and temporary structure, as insects will quickly infest the bark and migrate into the wood itself, which soon leads to decay and destruction. Peeling the logs is, by far, the most time-con-

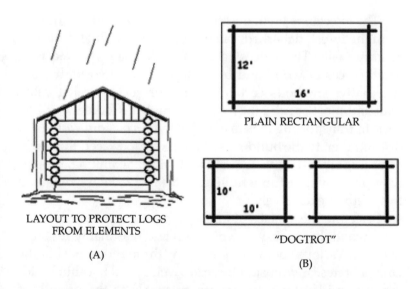

LAYOUT TO PROTECT LOGS
FROM ELEMENTS

(A)

PLAIN RECTANGULAR

"DOGTROT"

(B)

Figure 2-2: Elements of general planning.

suming and labor-intensive step, but without it your cabin is doomed to a very short life—about enough time for you to really get to like it.

Figure 2-2(b) shows two log cabin floor plans that I have built and used. The sizes shown are for the platform, or floor, that is made of standard lumber. The log walls are outside the platform and rest on the same foundation. The plain rectangular plan yields a floor area of 192 square feet, while the "dogtrot" design yields slightly more square footage in two sections. The dogtrot plan is characteristic of the Old South. In this plan a common roof spans two log frames, or "pens." The idea was to capture cool breezes in the days before air conditioning. The design also serves to limit the lengths of the logs needed to achieve those 200 square feet. This is very important when one is working alone and without heavy equipment.

SELECTING AND PREPARING THE LOGS

The log cabins I will describe in detail are made of logs cut from the forest, debarked, piled up to dry, and finally stacked to form walls. The spaces between the logs are chinked with small pieces of wood and brick mortar anchored with nails. Alternative methods certainly exist for sealing a log cabin wall, but most require the logs to be milled in some way. The costs of transporting logs to a mill that does custom work (few do) and then to the building site are likely to exceed those of a commercially available log cabin kit. Mortar chinking, properly applied, will last indefinitely, and I have always relied on this method exclusively.

Selecting the species of log is the next important step. We want wood that is easy to work with and reasonably resistant to decay. Various species of pine grow throughout most of the United States, and most of these are well suited to cabin building. The mid-Atlantic states are amenable to the growth of loblolly pine, which is actually planted there as a crop. This type of pine grows tall and straight and fairly rapidly. Landowners frequently replant harvested areas with a density that requires thinning after a dozen years or so. The culls are often cut up for pulp, but they usually also contain many suitable cabin logs. It is a buying opportunity worth investigating. Other conifers are good too, as long as they are reasonably straight and 8 to 10 inches in diameter. Some species have an inconvenient number of knots, though.

Another tree that grows tall and straight is the poplar. It is lighter and easier to peel than pine, and it dries more rapidly. It is more prone than pine to "checking," or the appearance of long surface cracks as the wood dries. Practically all species of wood will do this to some degree; it's a defect that must be lived with. I like to use a particularly decay-resistant species for the first course of logs (those closest to the ground). One such species that grows in the mid-Atlantic region is locust. This tree grows rapidly, but not particularly straight. It also dies quickly and then dries to become extremely hard and decay-resistant. It can be used as a long-lasting fencepost without chemical treatment. Zig-zag split rail fences made of it may be found standing after a hundred years. Locust has little commercial value, and people will often give standing trees away to be rid of them. However, a standing tree of the correct size, with dead limbs and bark fallen from the trunk, is actually a valuable, ready-to-use cabin component. Fallen locust trees are often salvageable as well, which is not the case with other species. Locust cut live must be used with care, as the thin layer of sapwood does decay and sometimes spreads decay to the usually invulnerable heartwood. Curves in the trunk will likely call for splicing pieces together to make up that first course, but the extreme decay resistance of the wood makes it worth the effort. Locust wood is so hard that it will also quickly dull your tools. Oak and cedar are other candidates for the first course, although oak must be well dried beforehand, because it tends to twist and warp quite badly as it dries. One species of "giveaway" wood that is hardly worth the taking is birch, which derives practically all of its decay resistance from its thick bark. Once that is removed, the wood decays very rapidly and the precautions mentioned above do little to stop it. Make a canoe from the bark and burn the rest.

Once you've found your trees, fell them, cut them to about the length you'll be using, and peel those lengths right away. That way you're ahead of the inevitable insect infestation, and the bark at this stage is easiest to remove. It is still a hard and messy job— particularly with pine. I recommend getting cheap coveralls and sacrificing them to the cause. For the size log we are talking about here (around 10 inches in diameter), a large drawknife does a good job with reasonable economy of effort. You'll be kneeling astride the log and getting dirty and sticky. There is an alternative tool that allows you to stand up, but I find it takes more elbow grease. That tool is the barking spud. This long-handled implement has a stout scraper blade at its end. (These are somewhat hard to find, but an acceptable substitute is an ordinary brush ax sharpened at its blunt end.) Switching between these two peeling methods will help keep you from getting too stiff too quickly. While doing this job, it's helpful to remember that you could be paying health club fees, doing about the same amount of work, and not getting a log cabin out of it.

You should haul your peeled logs to a location where you can let them dry. Set the pile on a couple of railroad ties (or decay-resistant log equivalent), separate tiers of drying logs with poles to provide air circulation, put poles or pieces of scrap lumber across the top of the pile (again for air circulation), and top it all off with a waterproof tarpaulin. Cover the top and enough of the sides to keep most of the rain out while still admitting lots of air. The stack should stand for about a year. It is *possible* to build a cabin with freshly cut logs if proper precautions are taken to allow for extra shrinkage, but the costs are great. They'll be much heavier than they would be after a year of drying, and they'll also be slippery with sap. Also, there's much to do before it is time to begin notching and stacking those logs, so plan your project to allow for drying time.

PREPARING THE FOUNDATION AND PLATFORM

The foundation serves to hold the ground floor and the walls above the decay-promoting moist ground. With most buildings, the walls rest on the ground floor, which rests on a continuous foundation. Not so with log cabins. In this case, the platform, which is best made of milled (and preferably treated) lumber, is set to rest *inside* the log walls on foundation support points, or piers, which also support the logs at their ends and at selected midpoints, such as under joints. (While other kinds of buildings are best built on a continuous foundation rather than piers, continuous support of the walls is a disadvantage with log cabins because it places support at the logs' lowest points rather than where you really need it.) To seal off the space underneath the cabin, a nonload-bearing screen of brick or stones is built between the piers. A single thickness of brick is enough for this low wall, which should have at least two louvered or screened vents to allow air circulation underneath the cabin while excluding forest creatures. You can also build the foundation of a log cabin with stones, using the same basic concept. If you choose this route, a stable stack of flat stones rather than a large block should form the weight-bearing piers; the horizontal cracks between the layers will prevent ground moisture from creeping up and contacting the wood.

The first step is to lay out the foundation using string and batter boards. This technique is illustrated in Figure 2-3. Batter boards are simple wooden frames, located so as to approximately frame the platform and driven into the ground so that their horizontal members are all at the level at which the platform will rest. You first adjust the horizontal boards until they

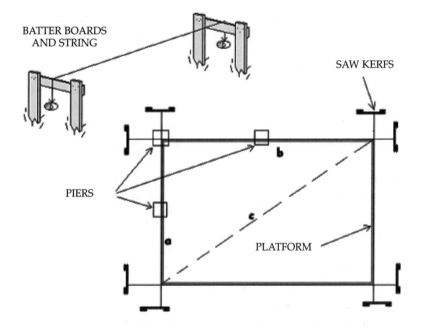

Figure 2-3: Laying out a foundation with string and batter boards.

are all level with one another while remaining horizontal. An ordinary carpenter's level can be used to keep each individual board horizontal, and to ensure that they are all at a common level, a sight level is very useful. This inexpensive tool looks like a palm-sized telescope. In its field of view is a horizontal line and an image of a bubble. When the bubble is even with the horizontal line, your line of sight is level, and you can use that fact to achieve a common level among the objects in your line of sight.

Once the batter boards are all at the same level, you can stretch strings, weighted at the ends, between them. Next you adjust the strings, sliding them across the tops of the batter boards until they form a perfect rectangle. To achieve proper right angles, it is best to use the Pythagorean relationship. If you are laying out the 12' x 16' cabin of Figure 2-1, then c turns out to be 20', a multiple of the 3-4-5 right triangle. If you are laying out one of the 10' x 10' pens of the dogtrot, then c turns out to be quite close to 14' 1 5/8". Once you have pinpointed the proper locations of the strings, cut saw kerfs in the batter boards. Now you can remove and replace the strings as needed while work progresses.

You are now ready to dig the holes for your piers (to a depth that ensures stability, i.e., to solid earth below the local frost line), shallow trenches for your screening walls, and possibly a hole for the base of a brick chimney. If you plan to include a chimney, it will need a separate concrete base about 18" square and 12" thick. You can place it anywhere you like inside the cabin, so long as it can stand independently and not bear any significant amounts of structural load. The easiest way to achieve that independence is to adjust its location so that it rises between floor joists and roof rafters and, of course, misses the ridge pole, which should not have any breaks along its length. (More on chimneys later.)

This is also a good time to remove any vegetation within the area of your foundation and treat the ground for termite protection. Now that the old standby, Chlordane, has been banned from the marketplace, the termite preparations that are available require that the initial application percolated into the trenches and holes when you first dig them be followed by "booster shots" every five years or so. The booster is applied by opening a shallow trench 2 or 3 inches wide along the outside edge of the foundation and percolating solution there. Some localities are loaded with termites and may requre more frequent boosters; local hardware merchants should be able to advise you.

It's now time to build your supporting piers and floor, and possibly the concrete base for a chimney. (I like to wait to add the screening walls until after the floor and first coarse of logs are in place.) First, line the bottom of the holes where the piers

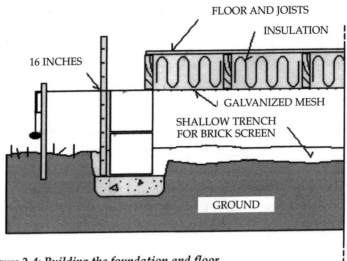

Figure 2-4: Building the foundation and floor.

are to stand with concrete and then build the piers up to the level of the strings (see Figure 2-4) using bricks or cinderblocks. (Cinderblocks can be greatly improved in appearance by *pargeting* the outside surfaces; that is, applying a surface layer of mortar with a trowel.) If you use stones for the foundation, you can line your holes and trenches with coarse gravel or railroad ballast rather than concrete. If you are including a chimney, you needn't be fussy about bringing the concrete base up to a common level below the batter board strings, as was necessary for the supporting piers.

There are methods of building a floor with log "sleepers" rather than floor joists, but they require a particularly large investment in time and effort. Having tried sleepers, I recommend milled lumber instead. I like to design the size of the platform so that the subfloor can be made of 4' x 8', tongue-and-groove, treated plywood. Floors are usually built with 2" x 8" (1.5" x 7.5") joists and headers. (More specific data on selecting proper commercial building materials may be found in various standard references, such as *Pocket Ref*, compiled by T.J. Glover. This handy, pocket-sized source of all kinds of practical information can frequently be found near the checkout counters at building supply stores.)

It is also a good idea to insulate your floor at this stage. The wood heat you're likely to be using won't warm up your feet very much unless you do. I like to use insulating bats supported with light, galvanized wire mesh. Figure 2-4 illustrates the location of the mesh. Without it, the insulation tends to sag as the years go by.

Once the floor and the first coarse of logs are in place, build your screening walls to fill in the space between the piers.

FABRICATING BOXES FOR WINDOWS AND DOORS

The windows and doors of a log cabin fit into wooden boxes or frames. These are plain to see when inspecting any log cabin. But there is an important subtlety that remains unseen on a finished cabin: to allow for the fact that the log walls will sink slightly as they continue to dry out, there are slip joints at the sides of the boxes and a telescoping space above. Without this provision, annoying cracks between chinking and logs will appear and demand repeated patching.

Wood dries in two stages. During the first, most of which will occur during the year we've allotted for our under-tarpaulin stack, the sap dries out and the log becomes noticeably lighter. During subsequent years, the cells that comprise the wood shrivel somewhat. As this happens, the log will lose some of its diameter while retaining all of its original length. For a pine log, this second stage of drying will take three to five years. A 10-inch pine log will lose about a quarter-inch of its diameter. There's no stopping it, and there is a benefit: the wood will become harder and stronger during that time. So you plan on your cabin's becoming a couple of inches shorter

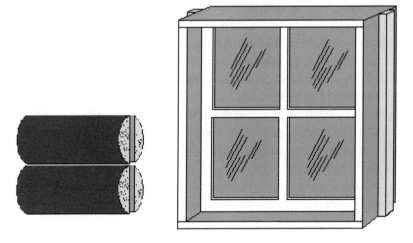

Figure 2-5: A window box.

in the long run, and your door and window boxes must accommodate that. Figure 2-5 shows how.

It may seem tempting to just spike the logs to the box and be done with it. But building the box as shown really isn't that hard. All you need do is attach a couple of 2" x 2" (1.5" x 1.5") cleats to the sides of the box and cut matching slots in the ends of the logs with your chain saw. As you build the log walls, remember to leave a few inches of headspace between the top of the window box and the log above it. This space can be filled with some crushable insulating material and covered with boards attached to the top of the box and able to accommodate the top log as it slowly descends. Of course, there is a corresponding consideration for the doors, the main difference being that window boxes are fabricated around a store-bought window casement, whereas a log cabin door is usually a homemade affair.

Our log cabin may have to be unattended for lengthy periods of time, during which hunters, kids, or other woodland wanderers may come upon it. We cannot count upon their benevolence. Vandals do exist, and they are in their most uninhibited state when alone in the woods. The best we can do is to make it very inconvenient for them to damage the outside or to get inside. That's quite a bit of prevention, really. Lazy and irresponsible individuals don't go about carrying heavy tools, and the outside of your cabin can present a formidable facade, particularly if you include the locking shutter arrangement shown in Figure 2-6.

Here is a top view of our window box with its casement in place. Heavy shutters swing on surface-mounted hinges attached to the outside that well-equipped passersby might attempt to unscrew. The would-be vandals will not benefit from their efforts, however, because there are locking pegs inside the jam and the center board is held closed with engaged threaded locking rods at top and bottom. The pegs fit into wells that are lined with a bit of iron pipe for extra resilience. The pegs are easily made by partially sinking a stout wood screw and then cutting off its head. The threaded locking rods, which run through channels cut through the top and bottom of the casement, engage a stout piece of metal

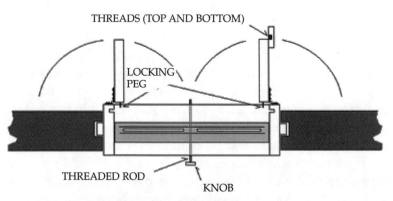

Figure 2-6: A locking scheme for cabin windows.

embedded in the wooden center board. This piece of hardware will probably have to be homemade; I have never encountered such an item in a hardware store. All there is to it is a 1/4-inch-thick, 3-inch-long piece of scrap iron with three holes drilled into it. The center hole is tapped to mate with the locking rod (I use 3/8-inch threaded stock), and the other two holes are chamfered so as to be screwed into a matching mortise. Or you can fabricate a functional equivalent from other odds and ends that might be on hand—so long as it's strong.

My cabins all have homemade doors. Most doors found at building supply stores are made for more civilized locations and could be beaten in easily. These doors depend upon the local cop on the beat for most of their alleged security. Some heavy boards and some Skil saw work will produce a door that is much stronger and also fits the rustic nature of the log cabin structure, Figure 2-7 illustrates my favorite plan. It begins with a tall version of the box with side cleats like those used for the windows. To build the door itself, three wide boards laid side to side are bound together with four 1" x 3" slats. One slat is placed at the base, while the other three are arranged in a Z configuration on the upper half of the door to prevent to it from developing a sag as the wood ages. Cracks will slowly develop between the three main boards if their edges are simply cut square. Cutting half-inch-wide ledges into the edges of the boards (with a Skil saw on a shallow setting), will give you "ship lap" joints that won't let the weather in as the boards shrink slightly with age. If you have the machinery to cut them or wish to buy precut boards, tongue-and-groove joints will also do the job. Assemble the pieces with galvanized decking screws applied with a motorized driver, and you will have a solid door with reasonable effort.

The door jam is completed by fastening 1" x 3" cleats to the inside of the box as shown. The door opens inward for security. I have found an ordinary thumb latch to be satisfactory, and for locking up I like to use a heavy-duty hasp and

HASP INLET TO SWING INSIDE

INSIDE

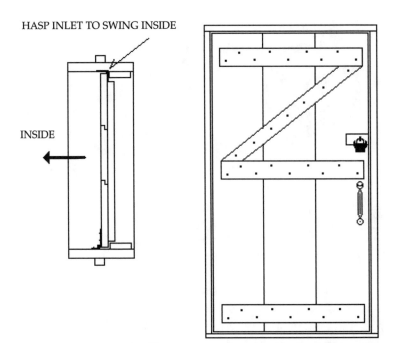

Figure 2-7: A homemade cabin door.

padlock. I locate the hasp so that its hinge pin is concealed within the doorframe, and I use an especially heavy padlock. Master makes a heavy-duty model that features stout ears to protect the shackle from hacksaws and bolt cutters. Any locksmith shop will carry it.

ERECTING LOG WALLS

Well, it's time for the main event—erecting log walls. I have had many visitors look at my log cabins and exclaim that cutting the corner notches must have been an exhausting task. Actually, it's one of the easier things to do. The hardest job of peeling the logs is now in the past. A tape measure, a carpenter's level, a lumber crayon, a double-bladed ax (or a large

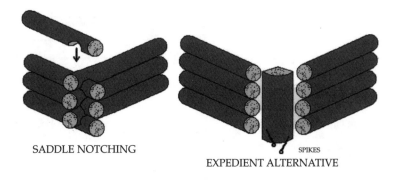

SADDLE NOTCHING

SPIKES
EXPEDIENT ALTERNATIVE

Figure 2-8: Two types of log cabin corners.

chisel and mall), and a small chain saw are the main tools of this trade.

When choosing a chain saw for this project, you do *not* want to select the biggest and meanest saw in the store. All that extra size and power will do is make you tired and deprive you of the high degree of control you will need. The smallest of motors with a 14- or even a 12-inch bar will do fine.

When it comes to choosing the type of corners for the cabin, I really recommend saddle notching over the expedient alternative. I mention the expedient only for those who have barely enough logs or are in a hurry. I have used the expedient method one time, I have seen the log cabin village at the historic mansion made this way survive for more than half a century, and I recognize its superior maintainability—you can replace an individual log in the wall if need be. The one thing that makes this method more difficult is preparing the quartered log used at each corner. This log needs only enough length to reach the ceiling, but it does have to be nearly twice the diameter of the wall logs. Making a straight rip cut with a chain saw is not easy. The teeth aren't designed for it, and this one task really needs a larger bar than the 12 or 14 inches recommended for the rest of the job. In spiking the corners together you will also lose the ability to make those door and window box slip joints work to your advantage. You might just as well spike the logs to the window and door boxes if you go with this method, and you will probably have to patch your chinking as years go by. The one time I used this method, I also used poplar wood, which dries quite quickly and does much more of its shrinking during the time it's under the tarpaulin. I have had relatively few patches to make. Enough said. Do it if you must.

Let us now address the task of constructing a log wall with notched corners. Many people have inspected my log cabins and expressed great surprise that the notches appear only on the bottom of the logs and that they are half a log diameter in depth. Evidently they had long ago played with the ever-popular Lincoln Log toy set, which uses lock notching; that is, notches a quarter log diameter deep cut in the top and bottom. Lock notching is certainly a recognized way to make a log cabin, and it is the strongest method of all. However, it gives you *no flexibility* in adjusting the corners after you have cut the notches. Saddle notches, with that half-diameter-deep notch below, enable you to slide the log from side to side slightly after it is in place. This is a very valuable option. There is no way to make a cabin of unmilled logs as straight and as plumb as a frame or brick building would be. The materials you have to work with aren't that perfect. But saddle notching gives you the wiggle room you need to approximate a plumb building as closely as possible. A plumb bob or long carpenter's level held vertically along the center of the log ends is your best guide. You must do the best you can here. The eye is quite sensitive to an out-of-plumb building, and once you've finished the walls there's little that can be done in the way of corrections.

Figure 2-9 illustrates the job of cutting a notch. The whole process begins with an inspection of the log pile to choose the appropriate size for the next log to stack. They aren't all the

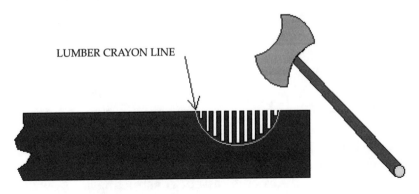

Figure 2-9: Cutting a notch.

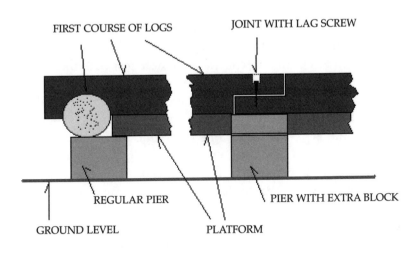

Figure 2-10: Joining logs end to end.

same size, so you must choose diameters and directions for their taper as you go along so as to keep the courses approximately level. The sight level is very convenient for this. Use a measuring tape and a lumber crayon to mark the limits of the notch on the side of the log where you will begin your cut, and then sketch the curved outline of the notch to be made. Now use your small and agile chain saw to make the series of cuts as shown and an ax to chip out the half-moon slices and smooth things up. A double-bladed ax is thinner than a single-edged one and does a better job. As a slower, less violent alternative, you may want to consider using a large chisel and mallet. Occasionally, it is convenient to join two logs end to end. This is particularly true for that first course of locust or other decay-resistant logs, which often aren't straight enough to make it in one length.

Figure 2-10 illustrates how to join two logs end to end in a way that is nearly as strong as a continuous length. It is a lap joint in which each log has a flat-bottomed notch, half a log deep, that extends in from the end about 10 inches. These are easier to make than the cup-shaped saddle notches because they require only three or four chain-saw cuts halfway into the log before a blow from an ax or chisel cleanly breaks the pieces away. A lag screw set into a deeply countersunk hole makes the joint really strong. The joint shown is resting on a pier and uses a short lag screw. If you use this technique to join a log that rests on another, an extra- long lag screw that extends down into the log below will give you much greater rigidity.

It usually takes two or three trials to get notches on both ends to fit properly. The retrials are no great inconvenience when the logs are still low to the ground, but as you near the top, lifting the logs to their proper place gets harder and harder. But there is a way. You don't have to be Hercules, and you don't need a crane. Fortunately, we are talking about a small cabin, and our logs have (hopefully) had some time to dry out

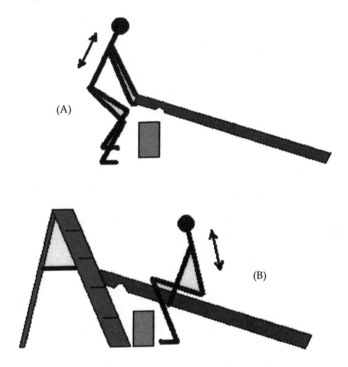

(A)

(B)

Figure 2-11: Lifting logs into place

and become lighter. Figure 2-11 shows some tricks that allow you to lift the logs into place alone.

It's not hard to find someone who complains of having a bad back. There are plenty of ways to injure your back permanently, and some of them are quite easy to do. Those involve a very avoidable no-no. You must *never* bend over, grab something (however light), and lift it by rotating your back up straight again. Backs aren't made for that. Your legs are. The stick figure in Figure 2-11 is in the process of lifting a log to a high position where the notch cut in the bottom of it will hook over the top of a nearly finished log wall. In (a) he is lifting one end of a log from the platform of the cabin (gaining the advantage of height over the ground level outside) onto an upturned cinder block. This is a short distance, so he can raise it by keeping his back straight (albeit tipped over slightly to maintain balance) and using leg power alone to lift. Arms do not flex here; they are straight like cables. In (b) the stick figure has moved a stepladder into position. Now he can find a point at which he can straddle the log and lift it up a step using pure legwork. Sometimes he uses a short loop of rope around the log (not shown) as a handle and a handy device for finding just the right spot where legwork will accomplish the lifting to be done. Once he's hooked that notch over the top log of a wall, the stick figure will move the cinder block and the stepladder to the other end of the log and repeat the process.

BUILDING A ROOF

As usual, there are several ways to do this particular job. Pioneers usually used horizontal supports called *purlins* and made the waterproof surface of overlapping handmade cedar shakes. This is a very nice way to do things. However, I believe that using some modern materials here constitutes a bargain in time and energy that can't be passed up. My favorite method is to use a kind of hybrid old and new technique. I like a log ridgepole with milled lumber rafters topped with lumber (or even plywood) topped with roofing material. To make all this, it is first necessary to add more logs to make up the gables. These are illustrated in Figure 2-12a.

Making the gables a tight fit to the roof is a bit tricky, since this is a place where round and irregular logs meet milled lumber. I begin by installing a small, vertical log center brace to the top three courses of each of the end walls to carry the weight of the ridgepole. I trim each brace so it has a shallow cradle at its top where the ridgepole will rest and 1/2-inch notches where it will meet the wall logs. Together with stout lag screws, these shallow notches help bind the braces to the end walls. I then stack small gable logs, perhaps

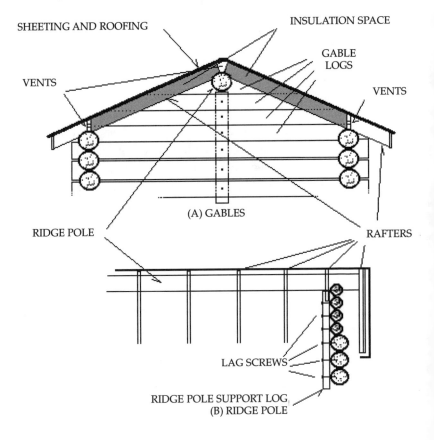

SHEETING AND ROOFING

INSULATION SPACE

GABLE
LOGS

VENTS

VENTS

(A) GABLES

RIDGE POLE

RAFTERS

LAG SCREWS

RIDGE POLE SUPPORT LOG
(B) RIDGE POLE

Figure 2-12: A method of constructing roofs.

two-thirds the diameter of typical wall logs and tapered at
the ends, from the top wall log to the ridgepole. Each is
attached to the vertical center brace with lag screws and to
the log below it with spikes driven into the tapered ends.
(See Figures 2-12 and 2-13.) It isn't particularly easy to get
these tapered ends to have a slope that will exactly match the
surface of the roof, so I do the best I can and then fill any

gaps that might be left with expanding foam insulation such as Great Stuff.

The rest of the roof is a fairly difficult job too, in that you want to have a tight fit between logs and lumber and you will also want a degree of thermal insulation. An issue that demands careful attention here is the potential for moisture accumulation and subsequent wood decay. To avoid that, you must cross-ventilate the chamber that contains the insulation. This sounds as if it's at odds with the whole idea of insulating a roof, but if you don't do it there will be an astonishing amount of water buildup as temperatures and humidity levels change. Enough water will accumulate to stain the walls and ceiling and to make you think there is a leak when there isn't. The absolute minimum amount of insulation space ventilation is illustrated in Figure 2-12a. Atop the side walls and between each rafter is a sealing board that meets the surface of the roof. Each of these boards has a 1-inch or larger hole containing an aluminum soffit vent from the building supply store. This roof construction doesn't feature a soffit (a horizontal panel below the eves), but the ventilation function must be preserved. Figure 2-13 illustrates a construction that will allow air to flow inside the peak of the roof. The rafters rest in shallow cuts made in the ridgepole so that at the peak of each rafter there is a V-shaped gap. I tie the tops of these gaps together with a band of sheet metal to hold everything steady until the roof boards are applied. Together with screened openings atop the ridgepole at each end, these gaps form exit vents for the moist air that always occurs when the outside temperature drops. The screened openings must be installed with care and precision, or they will become a favorite entry point for mice, bees, flying squirrels, and even snakes (I've had them all).

Another roof and ceiling scheme that provides more ventilation to the insulation chamber at some expense of head room is to place horizontal braces between the midpoints of the rafters on each side and have a flat portion of ceiling there.

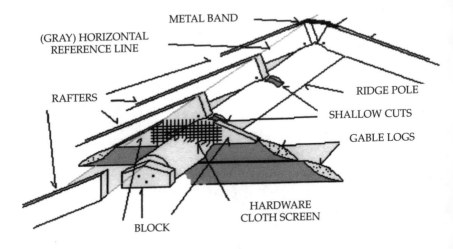

Figure 2-12: Joining the ridgepole with the rafters and the gable.

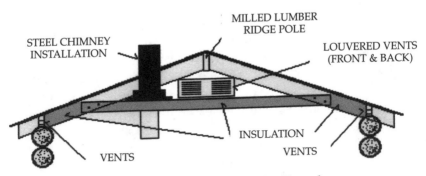

Figure 2-13: An alternative insulated roof and ceiling scheme.

The soffit vents still provide entry to air and the exit is now a pair of louvered vents in each gable just below the ridgepole. Figure 2-14 illustrates this scheme and also shows how this construction facilitates the installation of a steel chimney, an option that will be discussed later.

CHINKING THE LOGS

Working bricklayers call mortar "mud." Pioneers filled the cracks between the logs in their cabins with real mud. But that mud didn't last very long, and it also provided a home for various kinds of insects. Some modern factory-prepared log cabin kits use a specially prepared plastic mix for chinking. You can buy this stuff without getting a whole cabin kit, but it is very expensive, and each 5-gallon pail you buy won't go very far. This is because your logs were taken directly from the forest and have larger and more irregular spaces to fill than do the factory-processed logs of a kit. So I have adopted brick mortar as my log cabin "mud" of choice.

I begin the chinking job by filling the center of wall cracks wider than 1/2 inch or so with pieces of wood. I use a collection of long, thin pieces of scrap wood and a hatchet for this job. There are two objectives here: one is to save mortar and the other is to increase the insulating qualities of the log wall by blocking the transfer of heat that would otherwise be conducted by the mortar. The next step is driving a large number of cheap box nails partway into the wood at the edges of the cracks and bending them partly inward. I usually have a nail every 4 or 5 inches along the crack with some of them in the upper log. I also string some electric fence wire or other convenient iron wire along the rows of nails as extra reinforcement.

With the wood and iron in place I begin mixing up 80-pound bags of premixed brick mortar, not more than two bags at a time. The mud application job requires a regular-size mason trowel, a smaller pointing trowel, and a mortarboard. With my premix worked up to the same dough-like consistency used for bricklaying, I trowel two large dips onto the mortarboard and, moving steadily along a crack, I push mortar from the board into the opening with the backside of the pointing trowel. The pointing trowel is also just the right size for smoothing up the bead of "mud" before it begins to set.

Once the bead has begun to set, it should be left alone for at least a day. After that you can wire-brush away any slops that may be clinging to the logs.

Eventually, I brush the outside surface with a stain that also contains wood preservative. The mortar needs lots of time to set and dry before it can take this, however, so I apply the stain as the very last step of the cabin project. I also apply subsequent coats of penetrating wood preservative at intervals of about five years thereafter.

INCLUDING A CHIMNEY

There are several ways to include a chimney. A chimney with a fireplace is not discussed here because for the size of cabin we are dealing with, fireplaces are so inefficient for room heat that they are really just very large ornaments. A plain brick chimney *is* highly useful, however. I have built them in small cabins and have found them to be both attractive and practical. As mentioned earlier, they require a firm base set well into the ground with a top surface about 18" square and at least 12" deep. Figure 2-15 illustrates the essentials of a brick chimney. It is a simple stack or mortared bricks, six to a course, surrounding an 8" flue liner (as shown in the lower right inset). With a ready supply of bricks and bags of premixed mortar, building such a stack is quite easy as long as you have set up vertical guide strings to keep everything horizontal and square. The baked clay liner material, which comes in 2' sections, extends the entire length of the chimney except for a short section at the bottom where a cast-iron cleanout door is installed. A single upturned brick there supports the liner sections while the mortar sets. The middle section illustrated shows the junction of the flue with the clay thimble that accepts the stovepipe. You can get two of your liner sections with preformed cutouts to mate with the thimble. The inset at the upper right shows how these pieces go

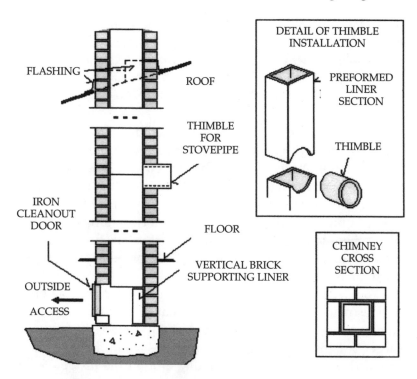

Figure 2-15: Elements of a brick chimney.

together behind the outer layer of bricks. Finally, the upper section indicates the aplication of flashing where the chimney emerges from the roof. I recommend copper flashing over aluminum, as copper is more durable and soon loses its luster, helping to keep the cabin inconspicuous.

I have also used manufactured steel chimneys. These are made of sections of double-wall stainless steel. You can get matching components to exit the roof with flashing built in, as well as a spark-proof chimney cap and a choice of bases. I have been happy with a base that is suspended from a flat section of cabin ceiling. It holds up the insulated stainless steel sections above and mates with a plain stovepipe from a woodstove below. These things aren't particularly cheap, but they are safe and take much less installation time than bricks and mortar.

INTERIOR FINISHING

For an inexpensive and attractive ceiling, I have settled on the following: With rafters spaced on 24-inch centers and with roll insulation in place (vapor barrier down), I tack in 2' x 4' pieces of drop ceiling material, perhaps made with decorative perforations. Drywall nails do a good job here. To cover the seams, I buy 1" x 3" (3/4" x 2 3/4") ferring strips, sand or plane them smooth, coat them with stain and varnish, and install them in rectangular patterns over the seams with small finish nails.

You will probably want some kind of flooring material besides plain boards or plywood. I have usually settled on a combination of tiled linoleum squares and pieces of remnant carpet bought cheaply from a carpet installer. I have usually installed painted pieces of molding around the inside of the window casements and included a small windowsill. A large brass washer protects the molding from the knobs that lock the window shutters.

Finishing the interior walls can be a bit of a chore, but if you stick with it you can obtain a very attractive interior at fairly low cost. With the interior side of the mortar chinking set and well dried, I vigorously wire-brush away drips and drops that have stuck to the logs. I then carefully scrape the logs clear of any bits of inner bark and lightly sand them. Next I apply a coating of boiled linseed oil. This will give the walls a deep luster. The application stage of linseed oil is a bit messy and stinky, however. Be sure to put plenty of old newspapers on the floor, or you will never be rid of the residue left by the drippings. The oil will take a few weeks to dry thoroughly enough for the final stage—a light coating of satin varnish.

Chapter 3

Campsite Utilities

When you are at home you are probably totally dependent upon externally supplied electricity, water, and sewage. Even with your own well and septic system, you need electricity to pump water. Electricity has become so reliable these days, even in rural locations, that it is very easy to forget how much dependence you have really developed. An interruption in service can lead to real inconvenience. Oil furnaces require both heating oil that you store and electricity that you don't. And our dependence on electricity pales in comparison to the degree to which we all take safe water for granted. Health departments monitor water safety so carefully that those rare cases of waterborne sickness are big news. If your cabin's retreat function is to mean anything at all you must learn to dispense with the use of these public utilities in ways that work and also attract no attention.

The log cabin retreat is first and foremost a camp. And when you go camping, perhaps without electricity, you probably make fairly frequent trips to the country store for ice, water, flashlight batteries, and the like. To have a campsite that functions as a retreat, you must give some serious thought to how you can keep on camping without making all those trips. It's a tall order, but it can be done. This chapter will tell you how, taking into consideration all of the following:

- Obtaining water
- Disposing of sewage
- Heating
- Cooking
- Lighting without electricity
- Utilizing alternative power sources
- Refrigerating perishable food

OBTAINING WATER

Safe drinking water has *always* been a problem. Ancient cultures tended to adopt one of two schemes to have potable fluids. One was winemaking. The ancient Romans handled wine, with its bacteria-killing alcohol, on a scale approaching that of today's industry, using giant amphorae as transport containers. The other scheme was brewing drinks like coffee or tea, which involved enough boiling to kill those germs. You really need to find a better and safer alternative, and you can do that.

Certainly the best option is to have a well dug on the property. But be very careful: there are likely permits involved. The well digger may handle all that, but if he must go to the authorities, that will raise questions. They will likely open a file to keep track of what is happening on your property. (KGB wannabees!)

My own practice is to carry in safe water for the vast majority of the times I visit a cabin in the course of a normal camping trip. I keep my other safe water facilities in a ready reserve state. Ideally, your campsite will have its own potential for water of some kind—an old well, a spring, a flowing stream or brook. You should avoid buying property with absolutely no source of water. The first priority is to make the source you have as contamination-free as possible. Old wells can be reinforced so as to limit the entrance of surface water as much as possible. You can isolate a spring from surface water to some extent by building a box around it and building up a berm around the outside of the box. Concrete is the preferred material for your box. Remember that treated wood has poisonous chemicals in it and that these leach out. Arsenic is often used, and its effects are cumulative.

Filters

Streams and brooks are the most difficult to isolate from surface water because they *are* surface water. And you can't be sure what is upstream. Livestock upstream can be a major source of dangerous germs. A shallow, hand-dug well near a stream will yield water that has been preliminarily filtered by the ground between the well and the stream, but it is still just a first step. While these sources are not potable, they will suffice for some things that require a large volume of water—laundry, some hygiene, toilet, plant care, and such. But for drinking, cooking, and brushing teeth, you need water that is free of disease-causing microorganisms. The old Boy Scout standby, so-called water purification pills, are no longer considered safe by themselves. These pills contain iodine, and although they do kill bacteria, there are also dangerous organisms that they don't kill. The worst is called *Cryptosporidium parvum*. It is not a bacterium but a one-celled animal encased in a microscopic cyst that protects it from agents that kill most other microorganisms. Another dangerous one-celled creature is called *Giardia*, which can escape a light application of iodine. Both are likely to occur in streams that pass by livestock or contain beavers, and both can make you very ill. And while there are antibiotic treatments for giardiasis, there is no such treatment for cryptosporidiosis. These illnesses will go away after several miserable weeks if you are healthy to begin with, but they can kill those with weakened immune systems (old people, recipients of any kind of transplant, etc.). What to do?

There are filters that render water safe from microorganisms. They won't remove dissolved chemicals (from industries, fertilizers, or nasty minerals in the ground), but they will filter out both bacteria *and* those pesky protozoa *Cryptosporidium* and *Giardia*.

There are several kinds of filtering devices available. The best look something like the stainless-steel coffee urn you see in a diner. The upper chamber receives unsafe water, and renewable filter elements at the bottom of this upper chamber trap all those harmful organisms and pass safe water on to the lower chamber, which is equipped with a spigot. The filter itself functions by the action of a special ceramic made from diatomaceous earth. The various filtering systems are rated in terms of microns (i.e., size of organism filtered; look for a micron rating of 1 or the word "absolute") and how many thousands of gallons of water they are capable of rendering safe. The larger systems use four filter elements, each of which is a cone about 4 inches high with a threaded pipe fitting at its base. The smaller ones are crockery containers instead of stainless steel and have only one filter element, and there are even portable systems with hand pumps suitable for backpacking trips. The premier manufacturer of these devices is British Berkefeld, which has long supplied missionaries and relief workers who use them to obtain safe drinking water in some of the world's most primitive environments. Competitive suppliers offer similar products, often at more attractive prices. (Some good places to start looking are included in the Source List at the end of the book.)

To obtain the longest possible life from these expensive filtering systems, you should clean up drinking water yourself before putting it through the final step of purification. A good way to do this is to prefilter water through paper coffee filters, which are cheap and easy to get. Another way to prolong the life of filtering devices is to periodically clean the outer surface of the filter element with an ordinary kitchen pot scrubber.

Ram Pumps

An interesting device that can *sometimes* pump water from a flowing stream to higher locations without electric power is called a "ram pump" (see the Source List for manufacturers). There is little new about these; crude ones first appeared in the 18th century. What is new about them is the economical use of modern materials. To use a ram pump successfully, you must have a stream that drops down at least 3 feet between two access points. The ram pump works by allowing water to flow down that drop distance through a long, slanting rigid (iron) pipe to the pump mechanism. The mechanism periodically interrupts the flow, using power from the water's momentum to create the water-hammer effect. The pressure peak that results from suddenly stopping the flow forces about 10 percent of the water upward, well above the level of the stream, while allowing the remaining 90 percent to flow on through. The pump mechanism and delivery pipe can be made of modern plumbing plastics. Note that you do have to beware of freezing. Flowing water will not freeze, but leaves and twigs stopping the flow can allow freezing and cause damage. You can deactivate and drain the system when you're away for the winter.

DISPOSING OF SEWAGE

Many of the laws authorizing the intrusiveness of local authorities originated with concerns about improper sewage disposal and the resulting contamination of water supplies. Unfortunately, the contamination of the integrity of those authorities was never considered. It is perhaps possible that a bunch of completely ignorant grade school dropouts living in a crowded hobo jungle could kill themselves off by lack of hygiene (as if we could be so lucky). But the laws assume that everyone outside of the government is that unenlightened. At any rate, you can learn how to make safe sewage disposal facilities as well as anyone else, so why not do it?

An underground septic system is best. You can dig it by hand, rent a Bobcat or other earthmover, or hire a heavy-equipment operator who is not a courthouse spy for the job. Anyone who can read can perform and interpret the percolation tests that must be done on the ground beforehand. Successful tests are often required before a piece of land is put up for sale, but do be sure to distinguish between a money-back guarantee that the land *will* pass a percolation test and verification that such a test has already been done. There are many reliable sources on a septic system construction, and although I have done it, I have no special expertise in it. Therefore, I will write no further on the subject, other than to reiterate that it is the best thing to do if you can. (A resource that describes the construction of a very minimal septic system is *Travel-Trailer Homesteading Under $5,000*, by Brian Kelling.) If you do opt for a septic system, even one made without local permits, guess what you'll quickly encounter? Another stupid, counterproductive government regulation! There is a federal regulation that limits the sale and installation of toilets to a new standardized version that is supposed to save water. It was promulgated at the behest of plumbing manufacturers who wanted standardization. They got more than they bargained for. The 'crats decided that there was a national water shortage crisis that had to be addressed. Thus, the mandatory standard uses so little water that it doesn't flush properly and often must be flushed again and again to get proper results, thereby using much more water than the old kind of toilet. Violators of the new toilet law are subject to many thousands of dollars in fines, but of course there is now a black market for new toilets smuggled in from Canada. If you can settle for a used one, there are old U.S. models to be had in "informal" sales.

There are some alternatives to a septic system if your campsite or budget is not amenable to such a project. Portable camping toilets that use chemical deodorants are quite practical in a camping situation. The chemicals are inexpensive, do a good job, and are readily available in large discount stores. They no longer contain formaldehyde, but they are strong chemicals nonetheless. One kind is strictly organic and works by accelerated bacterial action. The others are said to be biodegradable. The larger of the toilets are reasonably comfortable to use, particularly if you build a low platform beneath them. I have a closet-like enclosure inside my camping cabin, and the large portable toilet in it does not create an odor, even between cabin visits spaced weeks apart. I have an extra holding tank and an arrangement with a commercial campground with facilities designed to accept such waste. This keeps my ground free of waste and reserves its disposal capacity for true emergency situations. (Chemical toilet suppliers are enumerated in the Source List.)

While current prices peg a large camping chemical toilet at about $100, if you're willing to part with something like $1,000 there is another technology that is quite safe and does not present the chemical dumping problem. It is the composting toilet. Again, there are several kinds. Some are built in with a composting tank under the floor, some are self-contained but require some electricity, and others are self-contained without any electricity required. (The manufacturer of these toilets, Sun-Mar, appears in the Source List.) All require a vent pipe. Obviously, one requiring no electricity (for a ventilation fan) will not be quite as odor-free as one that does. Also, composting will grind to a halt when indoor temperatures drop to freezing and below. A possibility to consider is providing your own forced ventilation with solar-electric power (more on this later). I once discussed the utility of these toilets with a professor of civil engineering specializing in sanitation whom I met during a camping trip. She assured me of their efficacy and admonished me to be sure to "work closely with local authorities" should I choose to install one. I believe the technical evaluation but attribute the latter comment to typical academic naiveté. Finally, if you don't mind the smell or the additional risk of detection, an old-fashioned outhouse will also do the job.

HEATING

A previous chapter discussed the installation of flues without being too specific about what to use them for. Log cabins and fireplaces seem to go together like ham and eggs, but fireplaces are about the most inefficient means of heating you can choose. Two of my log cabins have fireplaces. One is a full-scale masonry fireplace with a Heat-Form steel damper and surrounding hot air channels. The efficiency is still terrible, and its real (and very occasional) use is to provide "atmosphere." This is not the stuff of an emergency retreat. Another cabin has a cast-iron Franklin-type fireplace with a steel flue. It is much better at heating than the masonry fireplace, particularly since it sits in the middle of the cabin rather than being in a corner or in a masonry well, but it still doesn't hold a fire overnight. In fact, very few cast-iron stoves will. The cast pieces don't fit together tightly enough to prevent air leaks from burning up the coals before dawn. Interestingly, being leaky like that exempts them from a new set of federal regulations aimed at particulates from fires having a highly restricted air supply (these 'crats can't stay out of *anything*).

In looking at modern—and federally regulated—wood stoves, you'll find there are several kinds. One meets

Environmental Protection Agency (EPA) emission standards by using a catalytic converter to burn off proscribed particulates at a relatively low temperature in the flue. Another is designed to pass flue gasses through a high-temperature region in order to complete the combustion process. The catalytic converter, as you might expect, has a limited lifespan and must be replaced. Naturally, these "pollution-control" measures cost lots of money and adversely affect the usefulness of the stove. Moreover, the substances being so carefully and expensively eliminated occur in the environment quite naturally. They are quite similar to the natural particulates that give the Blue Ridge Mountains and the Great Smoky Mountains the names they have had since their original discovery in Colonial times. Fortunately, there are people who bought welded steel woodstoves before these insane regulations appeared and no longer want them. Plain, welded steel stoves from a decade or so ago are very good. Their air entrances are easily and precisely regulated, and they are lined with special thin firebricks, which you can still get at woodstove dealers. Look for these kinds of stoves in newspaper ads or on Internet auction services.

A source of new stoves that will hold an overnight fire but escape regulation (by claiming to be strictly a camping item) may be found among the small group of suppliers to hobbyists who emulate the old fur trappers or "mountain men." A typical source sells "n-dog" stoves, where n represents the equivalent number of heat-producing dogs sleeping on the bed (see the Source List). These would be suitable for the smallest cabin you might build, such as one section of the dogtrot. The two main hazards of heating with wood are chimney fires and the overheating of combustables too close to the stove. You should get a chimney brush and use it once each year. Unfortunately, the pine that is so useful for log wall construction is utterly unsuitable for burning in a stove or fireplace because it will fill the flue with highly combustible creosote very quickly. A chimney fire can spread to the rest of the building or grounds, and even if it burns out unnoticed it can ruin the chimney's liner.

COOKING

Your wood stove might be a handy cooking appliance in the winter when it's going full blast anyway. Lighting up in summer can create much more heat than you want inside, however. You do need a separate cookstove. I like to avoid the kinds of camping stove that use disposable propane cartridges, as these tend to create a dependence on yet another store-bought item. I've found the good old Coleman camping stove to be the handiest thing to use in a cabin. The liquid fuel is something you must buy, but it is fairly inexpensive (particularly the generic brands) and lasts a long time. True, the directions say "outdoor use only," and there are some fumes involved, but I always have a window at least partly open and have had no problems. In fact, I have had a carbon monoxide detector present with nary a peep. I have not been happy with experiments with various backpacking stoves, finding them finicky and hard to light.

One "mountain man" camping item that will keep on working even during long periods of isolation from external supplies is the "brazier" (see the Source List). This authentic pioneer item is a stout iron box about 6 inches cubed with perforated sides, short legs, a handle, and a swinging top grate. It will cook very economically with lumps of dry hardwood or even charcoal briquettes. It is definitely an outdoor-only item, though, as glowing coals do produce copious amounts of carbon monoxide.

LIGHTING WITHOUT ELECTRICITY

Just about everybody has a kerosene hurricane lamp. They're not much to read by, though, and they smell of burned oil. There is one type of kerosene lamp that I've found to be very satisfactory (but not perfect). Called Aladdin lamps, these are styled for indoor use, feature a tall, slender glass chimney, and have a fairly complex burner assembly that includes a mantle. There is no pressure pump and no noise. A round wick partly burns kerosene deep inside the burner assembly. A skirt-shaped mantle above the wick catalytically combines those partial combustion products with additional air to produce a white light approximately equivalent to a 60-watt incandescent bulb. The mantle is very fragile and must be replaced after about six months of daily service. A mantle works very well during its lifetime, but eventually cracks appear, and as they grow it slowly crumbles. The whole lamp is an attractive home interior item and is well made. You can put away a modest stock of replacable items (mantles, wicks, chimneys, and little thimble-shaped things called flame spreaders) that will last for years. The kerosene must be reasonably fresh, but you can chemically stabilize it for storage with Stabil additive. (See the Source List.)

The only drawback of the Aladdin lamp is the possibility of a runaway soot condition. It will not burst into flame, though. If you try to turn up the brightness of an Aladdin lamp beyond its capacity, particularly when it has not fully warmed up, a small spot of black soot will appear on the mantle. If you notice this and turn the brightness down a bit, the spot will soon burn away. If you don't notice it, the spot grows and grows until it covers the whole mantle and also darkens the chimney. By that time there is visable smoke and noticable oder. So the rule is: Don't leave one of these going in a room by itself. Incidentally, a tiny pinch of table salt down the chimney of a sooted (but still burning) lamp will cause the flame to quickly consume the soot on the mantle (but not the inside surface of the chimney). This expedient will accelerate the eventual corrosion of the metal parts, though.

Curiously, the active ingredient of the mantle is the slightly radioactive element thorium. Thorium emits alpha particles that cannot penetrate skin or even a sheet of paper. Alpha emitters can be harmful indeed if the substance is retained inside the body. Not to worry, though. Thorium is considered quite safe (though not edible) because the body quickly rejects it. Dangerous alpha emitters are those that get incorporated into body tissues. The radioactivity has nothing to do with the light-producing property of these mantles. Coleman lantern mantles are made of the same material. When you install a Coleman mantle, you must burn it to a fragile ash before using it. An Aladdin mantle comes already burned and suspended in a wire frame. The burned mantle is coated with collodion, and the directions tell you to burn that off before using the lamp.

UTILIZING ALTERNATIVE POWER SOURCES

The most obvious way to get electric power without subscribing to a (blabbermouth) utility is to buy a portable gasoline-powered generator. These are very popular, and competition in the marketplace has resulted in some very attractive prices. Yes, there are times when the kind of capacity that a generator provides will be needed, such as when pumping water into a holding tank or operating power tools. A generator produces the many hundreds of watts needed for such tasks with reasonable efficiency and cost. In their own way, generators are very inefficient devices, however. The problem is that most of the time your electric power demand will be quite low. You'll have a lamp or two on and perhaps a stereo. Keeping a generator running for hours on end just for those is very uneconomical, and the noise is a great annoyance. Fortunately, there are other options.

One thing you can do is get a gas-powered generator for those heavy and occasional loads, *and* use it to charge deep cycle batteries for those long hours of light load. I will discuss batteries and appliances that use their DC power shortly. If you do get a generator, one feature that is seldom seen but highly desirable is a four-pole alternator. Most mass-market generators have a two-pole alternator, meaning that to produce that standard 60-hertz (Hz) power, the engine must run at 3,600 rpm. This is OK, but you'll get dramatically longer service from a four-pole unit that produces the same output frequency with the engine going at 1,800 rpm. There is much less wear and tear on the engine at that speed. The alternator itself is bulkier and more expensive, but a cheaper one that has to be prematurely junked because the engine failed is an expense too. You'll have to ask your supplier about the longer-lasting kind. There may not be any in stock because of the higher turnover of the high-speed kind. Due to the inherent limitations of storage battery service, I prefer to charge them by other means.

I recommend solar electric (or photovoltaic) panels for charging storage batteries. These are semiconductor devices with a large surface area that can convert sunlight directly to usable DC electric power. Their current expense largely confines their use to fairly remote locations (like your cabin), but one often sees them being used to run an intermittent load such as a school zone flashing light. Here, the expense of the solar panel and its rechargeable battery has become lower than that of tapping the overhead power lines that are usually already there. Applications of this kind are driving factory efficiency up and prices down.

Solar panels are commonly bought as arrays of cells (each running about 4 inches square) attached to a transparent, weather-resistant surface and framed with aluminum. There are tracking devices sold that cause solar arrays to follow the sun like a sunflower, but keeping something that moves out in the weather year 'round in good order can be a very demanding task, and so few solar installations use them. Usually an array is set up facing south and tilted at an angle that will make the best use of the sun's rays throughout each day of the year. Since the days are shorter when the sun is lowest in the sky, typically an array will tilt downward so as to intercept the sun during an early November noontime. This winter bias is easily made up during the summer with longer days. Each cell in the array produces a fraction of a volt, so numbers of them are connected in series to yield a voltage suitable for charging a 12-volt battery—typically 36 cells. The open circuit voltage of 36 cells is well above 12 volts, but maximizing the current delivered at battery voltage is the main objective here.

Twelve-volt lead-acid storage batteries have the advantage of ready availability and the ability to power a variety of useful electrical items (e.g., radios, kitchen appliances, and lamps) designed for cars or recreational vehicles. For lighting, there are several styles of 12-volt fluorescent fixtures that are actually more efficient than those designed for 120 volts AC. Twelve volts is not enough to run a fluorescent tube directly, so these fixtures contain a voltage-boosting transistor circuit that oscillates at about 15 kilohertz (kHz). It happens that fluorescent tubes deliver more light per consumed watt at these frequencies, so you get a bargain. The downside is that the oscillating circuit produces radio interference in the AM broadcast bands as well as shortwave. There is little or no interference at VHF television or FM broadcast bands. When I wish to listen to AM or shortwave, I turn off the fluorescent lights and use a high-intensity desk lamp. These lamps contain an automotive-type incandescent bulb that runs on 12 volts anyway, and they have a heavy base weighted with a 12-volt transformer. To make one into a battery-operated fixture you have only to disengage both windings of the transformer, keeping it in place for its weight, and wire the cord directly to the bulb. Then you remove the 120-volt AC plug in favor of the lighter plug commonly used for 12-volt DC appliances.

It is possible to use a large 12-volt storage battery to run modestly sized 120-volt AC appliances if you get an electronic device called an inverter. These things oscillate at 60 Hz and produce an angular approximation to the sine wave characteristic of both utility power and small gasoline-powered alternators. Very few AC appliances are affected by this change in waveform. Early inverters were quite inefficient, but more recent models have overcome that difficulty and, as another improvement, automatically shut themselves down to standby status when there is no AC load on them. Using high-powered inverters with such fancy features is really out of the league of a retreat cabin, so I have stuck with mostly 12 volts DC plus a small inverter that is used only occasionally. This arrangement is suitable for short-term heavy loads such as a microwave oven or longer-term, but lighter loads, such as a VCR. You can also get TV sets, VCRs, and combinations of the two that will run directly on your 12-volt supply. Most laptop computers will do this too.

Lead-acid storage batteries are a widely used but highly imperfect technology that has been around for more than a century. Their positive attributes are ready availability and the capacity to deliver bursts of very high current (thus their usefulness for starting engines). On the downside, they are very heavy, use a very corrosive electrolyte that may overflow or spill, and manage to short circuit themselves internally after five or so years of use due to a gradual buildup of sediment inside. For cabin use, whether charged by a gasoline engine-driven alternator, a solar array, or even a windmill (which I don't recommend due to the eye-catching motion), the lead acid batteries you choose must be the deep-cycle type. You do not want engine-starting batteries, no matter how large they are. The reason has to do with the number of times you can recharge a battery.

Batteries are rated in ampere hours. This rating indicates the amount of discharging they can take before they are fully depleted. Starting batteries and deep-cycle batteries may have similar ampere-hour ratings, but they differ sharply in the number of times they can be recharged. A starting battery, whose design is optimized for delivering high current in short bursts, can be fully depleted and recharged only about 15 times. That is why you can get away with leaving your car lights on overnight only a few times before having to get a new battery. Most engine starts require only a small fraction of the battery's full capacity, and the running engine can replenish that small fraction many times over. Deep-cycle batteries are the kind sold for trolling motors, golf carts, and floor-polishing machines. These can be recharged from full depletion more times than a starting battery, but we are still talking about only a few hundred times or so. Fortunately, you can discharge such a battery by 10 percent of its rating and recharge it again several thousand times. Cycles that are even shallower allow all the more recharges. The sediment problem shows up after about five years regardless of the amount of cycling, however. You can store a lead-acid battery indefinitely if you buy it dry and add the acid when you are about to put it into service. Trolling batteries are about the size of a truck battery. Six-volt golf cart batteries, each of which is about the physical size of a truck battery, are used in pairs to obtain 12 volts (and in sets of six in a golf cart), and the 6-volt batteries used in industrial floor polishing machines are the size of two golf cart batteries stacked atop one another. Floor polishing machine batteries are also designated L-16 batteries (for their height in inches). These monsters weigh about 100 pounds with their acid and are rated around 300 ampere-hours. An industrial distributor will gladly sell them to you with the acid in a separate container for easier transport. That's a good way to take them home even if you're going to use them right away. A good portion of the battery's weight is from the acid.

You need to keep your lead-acid batteries in a well-ventilated spot where their gasses can drift away without igniting. When charging, lead-acid batteries give off a small amount of a highly explosive mixture of oxygen and hydrogen. The thing to do is to be sure the gasses don't accumulate. This is easily done with cars, and you never hear of one blowing up. I keep my batteries in an underground chamber where the gasses can vent away and where there is little chance of freezing. Batteries are vulnerable to freezing only in a discharged state, but unanticipated circumstances could lead to that happening.

You'll want another electronic device between your solar array and your storage battery. This device is a regulator to prevent overcharging. If you continue to apply charging current to a battery that is already full, it won't accumulate any more charge, but it will give off a lot of that explosive gas mixture. Even if your venting measures take all the gasses away, this will deplete the electrolyte, possibly uncovering the plates and damaging the battery. You need only add water to replenish, but more gassing than that accompanying normal charging should be avoided. The regulators are relays that open and close according to a set of electronic rules, depending upon voltage and charge current. Some require adjusting voltage thresholds, and you need an inexpensive digital voltmeter to do that. Directions are included. There are other kinds of storage batteries besides lead-acid, and a good regulator can be adjusted to handle them. Most common among the alternatives are nickel-cadmium batteries. These, like the other alternatives, are quite expensive and difficult to buy, and I will not discuss them further here.

When wiring panels, regulators, batteries, and 12-volt outlets, you'll want to provide fusing and cutoff switches. Automotive fuses and fixtures are good for that job, but you must be wary of the switches you use. Anytime you throw a switch there is a tiny spark, which you may or may not see. Small as it is, it is still very hot and will melt a tiny amount of the contact. This is of little consequence in the AC switches we throw by the hundreds in a household because there is an

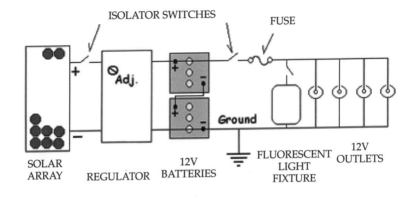

Figure 3-1: Small solar electric power system.

equal likelihood that the current is flowing in either direction at the instant of the spark. That way there is no net transfer of contact material from one side to the other. Not so with DC. Here the current flow and the melting metal cause eventual pitting of one contact and buildup on the other. That is why in the days before electronic car ignition systems we were forever changing breaker points in the distributor. So buy high-capacity, high-quality automotive switches and relays for your DC system. Figure 3-1 illustrates a typical system for a small cabin. Some suggested specifications for a beginner's system are tabulated below. A useful item not shown is a digital voltmeter to monitor the state of charge of the batteries. Pocket-sized digital voltmeters are very inexpensive and quite accurate. If you see the voltage drop much below 12 with no sunshine on the array, then it is time to cut off your loads until the batteries can recharge. If you suddenly see the voltage drop close to 10, then it's probable that a 2-volt cell in one of the batteries has shorted out and both batteries are due for replacement. A nighttime voltage of 12.2 to 12.4 under moderate load means your batteries are being well charged. An inexpensive electrolyte tester is also a good item to have on hand.

Sample Specifications:
- Solar array—36 cells, 100 watts (one or more)
- Regulator—Trace C-30-A
- Battery—(2) Golf cart deep cycle
- Switches—Automotive, 20A @ 12VDC
    Fuzeholder—Automotive, 20A @ 12VDC
    Light Fixture—12-volt fluorescent
    All wires—Automotive 10-gauge or heavier

REFRIGERATING PERISHABLE FOOD

There are four ways to produce cold:
- Ice
- Rankine cycle or compressor refrigeration
- Ammonia absorption
- Peltier or thermoelectric

Ice isn't all that good for a retreat cabin, although it is acceptable for camping when you don't mind making frequent trips to the country store. Before there was any kind of mechanical refrigeration, most towns had an icehouse, where winter ice could be kept for most of the year under a thick layer of sawdust. However, this is a very labor-intensive method of refrigeration, and it requires a considerable volume of storage space. I never seriously considered it for cabin use.

Ordinary compressor-type refrigeration is a highly mature technology, and there are many attractively priced products available in the size range suitable for a cabin. They would be fine if we were to allow ourselves access to utility power. But we're not doing that. There are 12-volt compressor refrigerators on the market, but a careful look at their power requirements quickly shows that a large, expensive, and conspicuous solar array and battery system would be required to keep it going. Economically, it just doesn't wash.

Ammonia absorption refrigeration is not quite as well known, but it is also a very mature technology. Units using this method are sold for use in recreational vehicles and trailers in sizes very appropriate for small cabin use. You will have to make an enclosure (open in the back) for these units, as they are sold with the expectation that they will be installed in a ventilated well within the trailer. Inside these units is a small flame that burns continuously. Usually it is a propane gas flame; modified units that burn kerosene are sold in the Amish community. There is a closed piping system containing a very strong aqueous solution of ammonia and hydrogen gas—two very nasty substances that you don't want to leak out. The flame is under a coffee percolator-like assembly that boils the ammonia out of solution. Cooling fins reduce the temperature of the gas, which is subsequently allowed to recombine with the separated water inside the cooling compartment. This recombination absorbs heat, producing the desired refrigeration. The hydrogen gas promotes the convection circulation that keeps all of this going without moving parts.

Overall, it is not a particularly efficient system in that much thermal energy produced by the flame is dissipated in comparison with the amount of thermal energy that gets removed from the cooling compartment. This inefficiency is usually considered acceptable because the cost of keeping the candle-sized flame going 24 hours a day is fairly low. A small, van-sized unit will run about six weeks on the kind of propane tank used for outdoor barbeque pits. The tanks weigh 18 pounds and hold about 20 pounds of propane. The refrigeration units do not last forever, though, even though there are no moving parts. There is a slow process by which scales form on the inside of the pipes and eventually find a small constriction to block up. Sometimes this can be temporarily repaired by a process known as "burping." You place the unit upside down in the back of a pickup truck and go about your (bumpy) business for a day or so. Often this dislodges the blockage, and refrigeration goes on for a period of time that is impossible to predict but often lasts for many years. Newer models contain an additive that is supposed to inhibit scaling. Unlike compressor refrigerators, where gas pressures are quite moderate, absorption units have gas pressures in the hundreds of pounds per square inch (psi) inside their pipes. These pressures demand that the pipes be made of heavy-gauge steel and be of welded construction. This drives up the price well above that prevailing in the compressor market. Some dealers for the main (overseas) manufacturers appear in the Source List.

There is something old and something new in the Peltier, or thermoelectric, cooling technology. The basic principle, discovered by Jean Peltier in the first half of the 19th century, is the old part. This French scientist discovered that when an electric current flows through a circuit containing two dissimilar metal conductors, a small amount of heat is pulled out of one of the junctions of dissimilar metals and deposited at the other. His contemporary, Thomas Johann Seebek, discovered that the flip side also holds: a temperature difference impressed upon two dissimilar metal junctions in an electric circuit produces a tiny electric current. The Seebek effect has long been used to measure temperatures (with devices called thermocouples), usually in an industrial or laboratory setting, and for the safety gas cutoff device used in any automatic gas appliance that features a pilot light. The new part is the recent introduction of special semiconductor materials in lieu of one of those dissimilar metals. The amount of thermal energy is no longer a miniscule fraction of the electric energy in the circuit. Picnic coolers are now available that use this technology and run on 12 volts.

The heart of these coolers is a tiny sandwich about 1 1/2" square and 1/8" thick. The "bread" is very thin ceramic with a copper pattern bonded to the inside. The filling is an array of tiny cubes (usually around 254) of a special semiconductor material called bismuth telluride. There are two wire leads that accept 12-volt DC current at about 50 watts. The sandwich absorbs about 25 watts from one face and discharges 75 watts from the other face at a temperature differential of about 54°F. Buying the sandwich by itself isn't a very good idea unless you have a well-equipped machine shop. Those kinds of heat fluxes get transferred to and from the sandwich only when there are flat-milled metal surfaces in proper contact together with a special heat-transfer compound. A manufacturer that has produced quality finished products using this technology is Igloo. This is not easy to do, and I have found some products by other makers to be less than satisfactory.

You have lots of choices to pick from for the various categories of utilities. I believe in starting each on a small scale and seeing how well your needs are met. For example, I have not become dissatisfied with my ordinary camping chemical toilet, and so I have not chosen to invest additional time and effort in something more elaborate. On the other hand, I did once add a second 12-volt solar panel in parallel with an existing one that wasn't quite giving me enough reserve battery power to last through extended periods of cloudy weather.

Chapter 4

Building It Bigger

(Four-Function Calculator Workout)

If you want to build a cabin that is noticeably larger than those we have discussed, then the only design issue that is not particularly obvious is the proper selection of materials from the standpoint of *strength*. This is a discipline within the world of engineering that can become very technical. This chapter will summarize, in a reasonably nonthreatening way, some elementary calculations that are of interest to the cabin designer.

If you build all or part of a structure from graded materials, then you may follow some well-known builder's guidelines or a commercial building plan and be assured that the various load-bearing beams you are using are strong enough to do the job. However, when you use a log as a load-bearing beam, you're on your own. Fortunately, the computation of the necessary parameters and the selection of the proper material are not all that hard. Figure 4-1 illustrates the basic problem in schematic form.

The logs that are stacked up to form a wall do not require

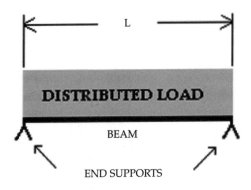

Figure 4-1: The uniformly loaded beam.

the kind of analysis we will undertake in this chapter, as they are supported from below along all or most of their length.

Most of the instances of a loaded beam to be found in a wooden building, log or otherwise, take the form of a beam of length L, expressed in feet (ft.), supported at each end and loaded throughout its length with a uniform load w, expressed in pounds per foot (lbs./ft.). This load comprises the *live load*, or the weight of those objects the beam is there to support, plus the *dead load*, or the weight of the beam itself and associated structural components. Most of the loads will actually be specified as area loads in pounds per square foot. These loads become linear loads like the one in the drawing when you multiply them by the beam spacing (expressed in feet). Think of each beam holding up an area of load equal to one half the beam spacing on each of the two sides of the beam. If the loaded beam in question happens to be a ridgepole, then the area load—comprising the considerable dead load of all the roofing materials plus a live load that will depend upon the anticipated maximum snow load—is multiplied by one-half the full width of the building. The one-half reflects the fact that half of the entire load is held up by the ridgepole and the other half is held up by the walls.

When the loaded beam you are dealing with happens to be a rafter, there may be a considerable slope to it. When we enter the beam length L into the formulas that will follow, we will use the horizontal distance from the ridgepole to the wall (as illustrated in Figure 4-2). The reason is that the force of gravity exerted on the load is strictly vertical. We are neglecting the leftover load on the eves. This may be done safely so long as the eves constitute a minor fraction of the entire length of the rafters. Actually, the load on the eves makes the load bearing a little easier for the rest of the beam by acting as a partial counterbalance. Eves with a very large overhang constitute a more complicated problem than we will address here, however.

Let's look at some of the loads a building must deal with. In each case, we are making a worst-case estimate. We will also be incorporating a safety factor, since the result of a failed beam can literally be the roof falling in. Table 4-1 presents some nominal values to use for the various loads that occur in a house or cabin. The roof specification is for moderate climates. If you are going to build a cabin in real snow country, then you should double the roof load specification, both for

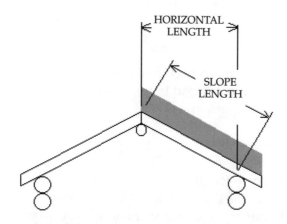

Figure 4-2: Rafter length.

	LIVING RM	BED RM	CEILING	ROOF
Live Load	40	30	10	20
Dead Load	10	10	5	15

Table 4-1: Nominal area loads for a house or cabin.

the extra snow load and for a steep roof slope, which will introduce a greater dead load.

We now need to convert these area loads into a quantity that we can use to rationally evaluate the beams that must support these loads. This quantity is called *maximum moment*, or *M* (expressed in foot-pounds). It represents the largest amount of internal torque that the beam must withstand. To get an idea of what "internal torque" means, imagine sawing a loaded beam in the middle and removing one of the halves. The remaining half will tend to fall downward, rotating about its fixed end. Now imagine keeping the remaining half-beam up, not by propping up the cut end but by applying a purely rotating force there. That rotating force is equal to that maximum moment *M*, previously applied by the half of the beam you took away. The formula for *M* is

$$M = \frac{wL^2}{8}$$

where *M* is max moment in foot-pounds,
w is the total uniform load in pounds per foot,
and *L* is beam length in feet.

The two tables that follow contain values of *M* for the four categories of service found in Table 4-1 versus several common values of beam length *L*. Table 4-2 is for a beam spacing of 16" O/C (on center), and Table 4-3 is for a beam spacing of 24" O/C. All values of *M* are in foot-pounds. If you have decided to double the roof load specification, you should now double the values of *M* in the roof column.

L (ft.)	LIVING RM	BED RM	CEILING	ROOF
6	300	240	90	210
8	533	427	160	373
10	833	667	250	583
12	1200	960	360	840
14	2133	1307	490	1143

Table 4-2: Values of M for 16" O/C beam spacing.

L (ft.)	LIVING RM	BED RM	CEILING	ROOF
6	450	360	135	315
8	800	640	240	560
10	1250	1000	375	875
12	1800	1440	540	1260
14	2450	1960	735	1715

Table 4-3: Values of M for 24" O/C beam spacing.

Now that we can find a value of M for practically any beam we may encounter, we must address the question of how in particular a beam is to support that value. We want to turn that value of M into a value of S, where S, expressed in pounds per square inch (psi), is the maximum value of fiber stress to which the beam material will be subjected. This quantity S will depend upon M and a quantity Z, or *section modulus*. Section modulus, which is expressed in units of *feet cubed*, depends in a complex way upon the cross-sectional shape and size of the beam. The formula for Z involves integral calculus and will not be detailed here. There will be three tables, however, that will yield values of Z for three useful cross-sections in a number of typical sizes. The first, Table 4-4, addresses rectangular cross-sections in the usual lumberyard dimensions. The nominal sizes (2" x 4", etc.) are tabulated along with their corresponding actual sizes (1.5" x 3.5", etc.) and their values of Z. Next, Table 4-5 indicates values of Z for square beams.

Here, actual side measurements in inches are tabulated. Measurements like 5.5″, which can be purchased as a nominal 6″ x 6″, together with whole numbers of inch sizes, which may be custom-sawn or hand-hewn, appear with their corresponding value of Z. Finally, Table 4-6 addresses various diameters of round cross-section logs used as support beams.

Nominal Size (in X in)	Actual Size (in X in)	Z
2 X 4	1.5 X 3.5	0.0017723
2 X 6	1.5 X 5.5	0.0043764
2 X 8	1.5 X 7.5	0.008138
2 X 10	1.5 X 9.5	0.013057
2 X 12	1.5 X 11.5	0.0191339

Table 4-4: Values of Z for sizes of dressed lumber.

Each Side (in)	Z
3.5	0.0041353
4	0.0061728
5	0.0120563
5.5	0.016047
6	0.0208333
7	0.0330826
7.5	0.0406901
8	0.0493827

Table 4-5: Values of Z for square beams.

Diameter (in)	Z
5	0.0071018
6	0.0122718
7	0.0194872
8	0.0290888
9	0.0414175
10	0.0568141
12	0.0981748

Table 4-6: Values of Z for round (log) beams.

For the final step in obtaining the value of stress S, there is the simple formula

$$S = \frac{M}{Z} \cdot \frac{1}{144}$$

where S is the fiber stress in pounds per square inch,
M is max moment in foot-pounds
and Z is section modulus in feet cubed.

Now that we have numerically summarized all the information regarding the amount of load, the length of the beam, and the cross section of the beam, the question has been reduced to whether or not a proposed material has the requisite strength to support that value of stress S. For practically any proposed load and shape of beam, *some* kind of material likely exists that will do the job. We are interested in wood, though. So the (almost) final step is to look at the amount of fiber stress various kinds of wood can support. We must see to it that the middle bottom third of our beam (particularly if it is a log) is free of knots, as these will significantly reduce the amount of fiber stress that the wood can withstand. We must also consider the species of wood. The final table of this chapter lists several species of wood that you might be considering for use in a log cabin together with their fiber stress (Fb), or maximum value of S sustainable by that particular material. (S is the stress caused by the particular load and beam shape. Fb is the maximum value of S that a particular material can withstand.)

If your chosen species of wood does not have a value of Fb equal to or greater than the S value for your load and proposed beam, then you must go back and change something, probably the cross-sectional size of your beam. If you've got that value of S covered, you're done! Put it up!

Not quite sure yet? Let's look at some specific examples.

Species	Fb (psi)
Gum, black	2000
Locust, black	4400
Oak, red	2500
Oak, white	2350
Pine, loblolly	2200
Pine, white	1700
Poplar, yellow	1600

Table 4-7: Maximum fiber stress (Fb) for various species of wood.

Suppose, for instance, that you are contemplating building a log cabin 24' x 24', and you would like to use the roofing plan of Figure 5-2—that is, a long ridgepole spanning 24'. Let us further suppose that you would like to use dressed lumber for the rafters. Let us suppose that the moderate-climate roof load specification of 20 + 15 = 35 lbs. per square foot (from Table 4-1) will suffice.

Let us first look at those rafters. Although each piece will actually be longer than 12' to allow for roof slope and eve overhang, for these purposes L = 12'. Let us first look at the possibility of spacing them 24" O/C. From Table 4-3, we see that M = 1,260 ft.-lbs. If we were to choose 2" x 6" lumber, then from Table 4-4 we have Z = .0043764. Our stress value S is

$$S = \frac{M}{Z} \cdot \frac{1}{144} = \frac{1260}{.0043764} \cdot \frac{1}{144} = 1999.36 \cong 2000\,psi$$

This value is likely to exceed the *Fb* of whatever species the lumberyard happens to have on hand—white pine, for instance. Suppose then, that we stick with 2" x 6" lumber but space the rafters on 16" centers. Now, from Table 4-2, we get M = 840 ft.-lbs., and S now becomes

$$S = \frac{M}{Z} \cdot \frac{1}{144} = \frac{840}{.0043764} \cdot \frac{1}{144} = 1550\,psi$$

This is more like it. Most lumberyard wood will meet this spec.

Now for that long log ridgepole. Our area load specification of 35 pounds per square foot is now multiplied times half the building width or 12′ so that

$$w = 35 \cdot 12 = 420 lbs \, / \, ft$$

This situation is not provided for in Tables 4-2 or 4-3, but we have our formula

$$M = \frac{wL^2}{8} = \frac{420 \cdot 24 \cdot 24}{8} = 30240 \, ft - lbs$$

Let us see if a 10″ log will do the trick. By Table 4-6, $Z =$ .0568141, so our formula for S yields

$$S = \frac{M}{Z} \cdot \frac{1}{144} = \frac{30240}{.0568141} \cdot \frac{1}{144} = 3696 \, psi$$

This is too much for anything in Table 4-7 except locust, and it is very unlikely that we could find a locust tree that large and straight enough for our 24′ span plus overhang for eves at the ends. Rats! Let's see what a 12″ log will do for us. For a log 12″in diameter, $Z = .0981748$, and our trusty formula comes out

$$S = \frac{M}{Z} \cdot \frac{1}{144} = \frac{30240}{.0981748} \cdot \frac{1}{144} = 2139 \, psi$$

Hmmm. A nice, straight, knot-free loblolly pine log can do this. But it's going to be a very heavy and unwieldy thing to raise up so high.

All this goes to show what you're in for when you build bigger and bigger. After all, most of the frame houses in any suburban development will have much longer rooflines than this, and they are unlikely to contain such a big piece of timber. The reason is, of course, that those houses do not contain such large, unobstructed spaces as the 24′ x 24′ area we're dealing with here. Those houses have numerous internal partitions and, most likely, prefabricated truss roofs. As a log cabin builder you have these options too, so long as you remember that your log walls will lose some height while drying and your internal partitions and supports must allow for this.

If you still want to think about a bigger log ridgepole, but not quite so big, try redoing these calculations for a 20 ′ x 20′ log building. See if you agree that 2″ x 6″ rafters on 24″ centers will have an easy-to-meet S value of 1,388 psi. Also see if you agree that for a 20′ span and a log ridgepole 10″ in diameter, S comes out, not entirely coincidentally, to 2,139 psi, able to be met by a slightly more manageable loblolly pine log than before.

Conclusion

I have been experimenting with building small, remotely located log cabins and outfitting them with self-contained utilities as a hobby for a number of years, and in this book I have tried to pass on the various lessons I have learned.

Though I started these projects with no inkling of what was to come, having remote places to go has become particularly important now that we as a nation face terrorist enemies who are apt to try using various means to contaminate populous areas or initiate epidemics of contagious diseases.

If you choose to follow my lead and build a cabin, please don't become your own enemy and hurt yourself by trying to do things in too much of a hurry. Felling trees and climbing ladders and hoisting heavy objects are safe things to do if you take your time and think about what might go wrong as you go along.

Good luck!

Source List

Many of the items you might need in the course of your log cabin project are not to be found on the shelves of your local store. Many are, though, as a wide variety of hardware items, camping items (e.g., Coleman stoves), and even logging chain are often stocked at Walmart, K-Mart, and other huge national chain stores. Other items are sufficiently peculiar that I have listed some outfits where you might start your search. I have no connection with any of them other than to have bought from them or to have had first-hand, satisfactory referrals. In most cases they are not exclusive sources for the items listed.

Automotive Suppliers

Automotive and recreational vehicle accessory suppliers like J.C. Whitney carry the sorts of electrical hardware and low voltage lighting fixtures you might need for a 12-volt solar electric system. They also carry a full line of camp coolers and ammonia absorption refrigerators. You may be able to locate some of these items locally at a campground or camping supplier. This can be an advantage in that refrigerators can incur heavy shipping charges.

J.C. Whitney, Inc.
1 J.C. Whitney Way
P.O. Box 3000
LaSalle, IL 61301

Composting Toilets
Sun-Mar Corporation
600 Main Street
Tonawanda, NY 14150

Mountain Man Camp Stoves and Braziers
Four Dog Stove Co.
25909 Variolite Street NW
St. Francis, MN 55070

The Log Cabin Shop
8010 Layfayette Road, P.O. Box 275
Lodi, OH 44254

Nonelectric Living
This unique store serves the Amish community and others who avoid the use of electricity. It offers a full line of wood stoves and ranges, Aladdin lamps and supplies, old-fashioned tools of all kinds, and an array of water purification systems. It is also one of the very few suppliers of full-sized ammonia absorption refrigerators.

Lehman's Hardware and Appliances, Inc.
One Lehman Circle, P.O. Box 41
Kidron, OH 44636

Reference Books
The Millionaire Next Door
Stanley J. Thomas and William D. Danko
Pocket Books
New York, NY, 1998

Pocket Ref
Thomas J. Glover
Sequoia Publishing Inc.
Littleton, CO, 1995

Travel-Trailer Homesteading Under $5,000
Brian Kelling
Loompanics Unlimited
Port Townsend, WA, 1995

Ram Pumps
The Ram Co.
HCR 61, Box 16
Lowesville, VA 22951

Home Survival
145 Sunshine Drive
Decherd, TN 37324

Solar Electric System Components
Two suppliers are listed here. Each has a large selection of solar panels, charge regulators, inverters, and other electrical components you might need. They also carry lead acid batteries. Before ordering batteries from afar, however, it pays to see what you can get locally. Exide and other brands have nationwide networks of warehouses, some of which will sell directly to the consumer. That way you can avoid heavy shipping charges and also carry in old cores for cash credit.

Sunelco
The Sun Electric Company
100 Skeels Street, P.O. Box 787
Hamilton, MT 59840

Real Goods
966 Mazzoni Street
Ukiah, CA 95482

Sporting Goods
Like many well-stocked sporting goods stores, Cabella's stocks chemical toilets and related supplies, portable water purification systems, Coleman camp stoves and fuel, and camp coolers, including the new Igloo thermoelectric types.

Cabella's
400 E. Avenue A
Oshkosh, NB 69190

Water Purification Systems
British Berkefeld does not sell directly to consumers. Entering the name into an Internet search engine will produce a number of dealers. Among them is

911 Water Systems
6225 Foxwood Trail
Birmingham, AL 35242

A less expensive brand, made of earthenware rather than stainless steel, may be found at

Epic Water Systems
EPI Corporation
RR 2 Box 318 B
Frisco, TX 75034

Portable ceramic water filters are available from other suppliers, including Cabella's and Lehman's, listed above.

About the Author

Michael Mulligan has built a career in engineering while pursuing hobbies centered around the reproduction of American Frontier artifacts such as the kentucky rifle and, above all, the log cabin.

He began more than 30 years ago by building a full-size home from locally cut pine trees and went on to build a series of smaller log buildings, including vacation and hunting/camping cabins. This book is a distillation of the many lessons he learned along the way.

Mulligan is currently involved in the research and development of improved ways of supplying remote locations with economical and reliable solar electric power.